P9-BZY-766

REVOLUTION IN LEADERSHIP

Ministry for the Third Millennium
Edited by Lyle E. Schaller

REVOLUTION IN LEADERSHIP

Training Apostles
for Tomorrow's Church

REGGIE MCNEAL

ABINGDON PRESS / Nashville

REVOLUTION IN LEADERSHIP
Training Apostles for Tomorrow's Church

Copyright © 1998 by Abingdon Press

All rights reserved.

No part of this work may be reproduced or transmitted in any form or by any means, electronic or mechanical, including photocopying and recording, or by any information storage or retrieval system, except as may be expressly permitted by the 1976 Copyright Act or in writing from the publisher. Requests for permission should be addressed in writing to Abingdon Press, 201 Eighth Avenue South, Nashville, TN 37203.

Library of Congress Cataloging-in-Publication Data

McNeal, Reggie.
    Revolution in leadership : training apostles for tomorrow's church / by Reggie McNeal.
      p. cm.—(Ministry for the third millennium)
    Includes bibliographical references.
    ISBN 0-687-08707-4 (alk. paper)
    1. Christian leadership.   2. Christian education.   I. Title.
II. Series.
BV652.1.M43   1998
230

To Paul, Brad, Walter,
and Jim . . . learning leaders

CONTENTS

FOREWORD

Once upon a time congregational leaders talked about "Christian education," "church buildings," "preachers," and "choirs." The conventional wisdom declared that a congregation with a superb preacher, an outstanding adult choir, an excellent Sunday school, and modern physical facilities enjoyed the essentials required to reach new generations of churchgoers. As congregations increased in size and as life became more complicated, they usually added skilled, paid staff to that formula. The first staff member often was a professionally trained Christian educator, a second could be a minister of music, a third could be a youth minister, and the fourth might be the business administrator or an associate minister.

That model often was an effective approach to ministry through the first seven or eight or nine decades of the twentieth century. Four recent changes, however, have challenged that traditional approach. One is the shrinking number of people who want to be taught by an expert accompanied by the rapid increase in the number of adults who are hungry to learn. Overlapping that is the recognition that knowledge—not money, physical facilities, an inspiring tradition from the past, or academic credentials—constitutes the most important asset in responding to the needs of people. Mastery of the knowledge-building process is the crucial ingredient that separates the effective organization from the ineffective one.

The third change is the recognition that teams, or what Warren Bennis calls "Great Groups," are the best way to meld together wisdom, experience, genius, creativity, and knowledge. The old pattern of individuals working alone in their own isolated empires is being replaced by teams. This change can be seen in farming, the practice of medicine, churches, manufacturing plants, construction, and almost every field except higher education.

The combination of these three changes introduces the fourth. What is the most effective strategy for creating apostolic leaders in the churches? The answer to that question is the central theme of this creative book. Bring together a team of people who are hungry to learn in an environment designed around mastery of the knowledge-building process. In simple terms, create learning communities. Instead of urging a pastor to return to seminary for another degree, encourage that pastor to help create and participate in a new learning community.

Does this mean writing off all the assets accumulated in today's theological schools? Not necessarily. That choice will be made, one-by-one, by each seminary. A more attractive alternative, that also represents good stewardship, would be to implement what is proposed in chapter 7. Transform today's seminaries into learning communities. That will not be easy!

More important is another question. How can you, dear reader, benefit from this revolution in leadership? The first step is to believe a revolution is needed and already underway. The Introduction and the first two chapters of this book should convince you that time has come. We can learn from one another! The teaching church and the learning community are two outstanding products of this revolution in learning.

The second step is to become acquainted with a new model. Every year thousands of congregational leaders, both clergy and lay, spend a few days learning from the experiences of the contemporary teaching churches. Every day new learning communities are being created by a group of pastors eager to learn from one another.

The third and fourth chapters explain the nature of a learning community designed to produce apostolic leaders. The third step is to ask, How can I join this revolution? The remaining chapters in this book plus the appendix provide the help you need to propel you down the road to a revolution in learning.

Join the revolution and have fun while you learn and grow!

Lyle E. Schaller
Naperville, Illinois

INTRODUCTION
THE LEADERSHIP VACUUM

Americans are suffering from a lack of leadership. This leadership vacuum poses more than a challenge. It threatens our continued existence as a society. Warren Bennis, respected author on the subject of leadership and founder of The Leadership Institute at the University of Southern California, observes that the leadership deficit is dangerous and global:

> Humanity currently faces three extraordinary threats: the threat of annihilation as a result of nuclear accident or war, the threat of a worldwide plague or ecological catastrophe, and a deepening leadership crisis in most of our institutions. Unlike the possibility of plague or nuclear holocaust, the leadership crisis will probably not become the basis for a best-seller or a blockbuster movie, but in many ways it is the most urgent and dangerous of the threats we face today, if only because it is insufficiently recognized and little understood.[1]

This leadership crisis affects every level of our society. Its most telltale sign is the appalling dearth of new ideas or compelling visions of solutions to problems facing our culture. The explosion of technology and information is accompanied by an implosion of will and courage demonstrated by leaders who fail to persuasively challenge human beings to new levels of achievement. Whether you look to the business, the educational, or political sector, the leadership landscape looks remarkably barren.

The church seems in no better shape than the rest of the culture. Less than one-third of pastors identify themselves as having the gift of leadership. Most confess to being teachers (52 percent), but few teachers really understand leadership and how it works.[2] Little wonder, then, that most congregations suffer the fate of leaderless organizations: lack of vision, loss of mission, and, eventually, loss of the ability to sustain themselves.

The impact of the leadership deficit in the church can be assessed in several ways. Church attendance is dwindling and erratic. While surveys of worship attendance indicate that total adult participation in American churches is at an all-time high, the percentage of adults in church on the typical weekend has declined for the past dozen years.

The evangelism picture is also alarming. Many congregations report evangelism rates that represent a decreasing market penetration of the gospel. This results, in part, from the church's interface, or lack of it, with culture. Many congregations have become sociologically cocooned, evidencing little interest in reaching beyond their family or tribe, however defined.

These danger signs raise questions about leadership. While many different solutions can be offered to turn this picture around, the underlying concern will return to the need for leadership. Persuasive arguments can be made for a need for a renaissance in biblical and spiritual worship, for instance, and in the renewal potential of small group applications in ministry and discipleship. These and other suggestions to church revitalization, however, do not get out of the box without leadership. There is not a shortage of ideas. There is a shortage of will exercised and called out by inspiring leaders.

A revolution in leadership is required for the renewal of the North American church. We must have different leadership than we are used to if we want better results than we are getting. Current leadership is proving inadequate to meet the current, much less future, challenges facing the church.

Leadership quality will not improve unless the process for developing leaders is transformed. Academic institutions are organized to reproduce scholars, not leaders. Traditional training methodologies are not producing competent leaders with the requisite skills for leading God's people into the third Christian millennium. Unless something is done to address this leadership deficiency, the Christian movement in our culture faces marginalization as a player of any influence.

Scripting a Better Future

Several key ideas drive this book. The first, already surfaced, is the presenting issue of the need for leadership competence to secure a better future for the church. We simply must have better leaders.

Second, raising the level of church leadership is not going to be easy. If it were easy, it would already have been done! Bill Hybels relates a story of a business friend who wants to relax in retirement by leading a church. "I told him," Hybels recalls, "that leading a church will ruin his retirement, because the church demands a higher and more complex form of leadership than business does."[3] We are going to have to ask the hard questions about how we train leaders, what we expect from leaders, and what leaders need to focus on.

Third, we cannot afford to hide behind the notion that leaders are born. Such a view leads us to conclude, therefore, that trying to train leaders is a wasted effort. No one will deny that some individuals have greater innate leadership abilities and gifts. Yet merely relying on these individuals to emerge and wield influence (especially in the oftentimes leadership-hostile environment of the local congregation) is an inappropriate response to the leadership vacuum. In fact it is just this sort of approach that has contributed to the present crises. Peter Drucker says it well: "There may be 'born leaders,' but there surely are far too few to depend on them. Leadership must be learned and can be learned."[4]

Fourth, the kind of leader necessary for the renewal of the North American church will be a different animal than what currently exists in most churches. An accompanying idea to this assertion is that a different model will need to be employed in developing a different kind of leader. We need to identify both the characteristic traits of new, effective leadership and how they can be fostered.

It is time for a new model of leadership and leadership development to emerge. Both elements are needed. Different leaders will require a different development methodology. Any new model must address both of these concerns. This book offers one answer to the search for this new model. The proposal in these pages focuses on the twin focal points of (1) apostolic leadership and (2) the learning community.

The new leadership called for throughout this volume is described as apostolic leadership, or leadership for a new apostolic era. In our day, an era that resembles in many remarkable ways the age of Christian beginnings, the same kind of leader is needed that the early church enjoyed. In short, we need apostolic leaders!.

The new methodology for developing apostolic leaders involves an intentional process called the learning community. Early apostles were effective because they were gripped by the Great Mission, empowered by the Holy Spirit, and depended on one another. They leaned on each other and learned from each other's experiences. By designing and deploying a peer mentoring process, we can help to address the church's need for developing apostolic leadership. This process of creating learning communities described in these pages fosters the emergence of leaders for a new apostolic era.

Apostolic leadership is an idea whose time has come again.

1.

APOSTOLIC LEADERSHIP

T he call in the church today is for apostolic leadership. What does "apostolic" mean? What significance compels its use for describing the kind of leadership the church needs for the future? Why recall the past when considering how to embrace the twenty-first century?

These questions can be answered with three assertions. First, the dynamic of the early church during the apostolic era remains a benchmark for missional effectiveness. Second, the cultural arena at the beginning of the twenty-first century resembles at key points the cultural setting that first-century Christians faced. Third, and most significantly, the type of leadership the apostles practiced possesses certain qualities that not only made the early church effective but would raise the level of church leadership today as we face similar challenges and opportunities. We will look at all three of these declarations in this chapter. Most of the discussion will focus on the third component, the leadership issue.

Early Church Dynamic Parallels

The rise and development of the Christian church cannot be described as anything other than a phenomenon. Historians and sociologists join theologians in recognizing that the human experience was reshaped approximately two millennia ago by a movement launched in Palestine. During the age of the apostles, a remarkable growth occurred in the number of believers in the geographic areas affected by the advent of Christianity. In two generations the movement leapt out of its geographic, religious, and ethnic origins to sweep across the Roman empire. Within two centuries, it found its way east to the edge of the known world.

The apostles presided over the explosion of the gospel that moved out from Jerusalem, to Judea, to Samaria, and then to the world, just as Jesus had predicted (Acts 1:8). In a more dramatic development, the movement burst the wineskins of first-century Pharisaic Judaism and spilled into the Gentile world, washing all the way to the emperor's household in Rome.

Those early disciples grabbed hold of the new commission given them by Jesus and turned it into the Great Commission (Matthew 28:19-20). They practiced their faith in a way that demonstrated the priority they gave to that commandment. Apostolic-age believers adopted the spread of the gospel as their marching orders. In the face of skepticism, unbelief, and hostility, they courageously shared their faith—with stunning results. Their fervor launched a movement that gained momentum in its early centuries. Between A.D. 250 and 350, the number of Christians increased dramatically from 1.7 million to 33.8 million.[1]

This pronounced growth characterized the expression of apostolic age Christianity. Any resurgence of this missional and expansionist dynamic in subsequent centuries has always been linked back to this distinguishing feature of New Testament church life. Periods of great revival and harvest throughout the two Christian millennia have often been characterized as outbreaks of the Pentecostal power detailed in the book of Acts.

George Hunter III, in his observations about reaching the unchurched, confirms this contemporary connection with an ancient past. He uses the term "apostolic congregations" for those contemporary churches that are effectively reaching unchurched people. In other words, when he speaks in terms of kingdom expansion dynamics, he resorts to the term "apostolic."

Hunter sees three similarities between the ancient world and today—all three relating to harvest potential. First, he contends that the increasing secularization of the West, coupled with the demise of an Enlightenment world view, has created the potential for a huge harvest once again. People are seeking a satisfying worldview that includes spiritual fulfillment. Second, the church has trouble perceiving the harvest, and most churches will fail to reap the harvest around them. Operating from a Christendom paradigm, the church's efforts focus primarily on the nurture and care of existing Christians, as though most people around them are believers. Third, too few laborers are involved in gathering the harvest. Evangelism in most churches means asking church members to share their faith and invite people to church events and activities. Little of either ever happens.

In response to this situation, Hunter maintains, God in the 1970s began raising up apostolic congregations. These churches target unchurched people with their ministries. They once again embrace the Great Commission as their primary focus, with an accompanying emphasis on lay ministry. They seek to be culturally relevant and practical in scriptural application.

Interestingly, in an interview recorded for *Next,* a publication of Leadership Network, Hunter admitted that more attention needs to be paid to the leadership issue for apostolic churches.[2] These congregations will require leadership radically different from the style required by Christendom congregations.

Cultural Parallels

A second parallel between the first-century era and ours involves several cultural similarities shared by the two periods.

Globalism. First-century Christians operated in a world that, for the first time in human history, had a sense of globalism. Palestine at the time of Christ enjoyed a polycultural mixture of Greek,

Roman, Jewish, and Eastern influences. The Greeks had given the world its first common language and a common political structure centered in the city-state. The Romans developed the transportation infrastructure during the *Pax Romana,* the five hundred years of world peace secured through Roman hegemony. Their military muscle provided the security for road-building, which in turn furthered the development of commerce. The roads, of course, ran both ways; and Eastern influence, especially religious, became widespread throughout the empire.

The Christian church was born amid this cultural diversity (Acts 2:9-11) and quickly spread to multiple cultural venues. The coming of the Spirit at Pentecost reflected the strategic timing of God to insure an immediate global impact. Jewish pilgrims to Jerusalem would fan out east and west, even south and north, telling others what they witnessed. The book of Acts records the spread of the faith—along Roman roads connecting old Greek cities—to Gentile populations.

That we are today members of a global community is not news. This is a fact. What began as a growing reality first in terms of economic development with the rise of multinational corporations has exploded into every arena with the advent of the cyberspace information highway. People are literally only a few keystrokes removed from any point on the planet.

Today, as in the first century, cultural diversity makes fertile ground for gospel sowing and reaping. The challenge for North American Christianity involves a willingness to emerge from a sociological cocoon and adopt a missional agenda designed to embrace the world.

Religious pluralism. Cultural diversity brought to the first Christians a challenge we now face as well—religious pluralism. Apostolic era disciples took on cults and state religions in the religious marketplace, as well as "mainline" religions like Judaism. Contenders represented a wide divergence of worldviews. Not suffering from the delusion that they were in charge or the expectation of having cultural props, first-century believers did not wilt in the face of competition.

Christianity is not the only game in town anymore. The influx of Eastern mysticism and Islam, the growth of Mormonism and various other cults, and the rise of secularism have combined to reshape the American religious landscape in the last half century. These forces outside of Christianity are perhaps bested in impact by a development within the Christendom worldview. Increasingly among Christians, moralism has replaced salvation as the hoped-for and desired outcome for those outside the faith. This may prove to be the most formidable foe of all for Evangelicalism. American civil religion has emerged as a moralism masquerading as Christianity, but it lacks the power of the real article to change lives from the inside out.

Early Christians faced a hostility to the religious exclusivism they injected into the spiritual milieu of the first century. Sometimes they faced persecution and even death for their radical views in this regard. Modern Christians seem perplexed when their worldview is challenged. Denial (with its telltale sign being a loud and vociferous cry for a return to the Christendom world order) or withdrawal constitute two prevalent responses that many congregations and denominations adopt in the face of this new reality. An apostolic approach would involve a commitment to and practice of engaging people in culturally relevant ways. A new apologetics is called for that recognizes that many unchurched people are not beginning their search from a Christian perspective.

Heightened spiritual awareness. First-century believers and contemporary ones share another similar religious frontier. Christianity emerged in a time of the collapse of traditional religion and a disaffection on the part of many people toward institutional expressions of spirituality. Seekers no longer believed in mythological pantheons nor did they trust state religions for their deliverance. The search for personal salvation and transrational mystical experience fueled a revival of ancient, Eastern mystery cults. Mithraism and Gnosticism posed a far greater challenge to first-century Christianity than did any form of emperor worship or mythology.

A variety of indicators points to the existence of much the same spiritual climate in North America. This culture is highly interested in spiritual matters. The connection, however, between the spiritual life and church escapes more and more people. Only 8 percent of Americans say they do not believe in either God or Jesus Christ. Thirty percent of those who say they are Christians never attend church. Overall church attendance is down for the last few years. Thirty-eight percent of church-going Americans attend church less frequently than they did five years ago; half of those who go show up less than once per month. A chief complaint of those who are dropping out of church is that church is not spiritual enough!

A scan of television shows, radio programs, book titles, and movie themes reveals a huge interest in the spiritual dimensions of life. But no longer do people equate spiritual with Christian—and certainly not with institutional forms of it. In fact, the church is turning people off. In 1995, only 20 percent of unchurched people said they would attend church if asked, down from 40 percent just ten years earlier. The most disturbing piece of information may rest in the numbers that report that 91 percent of seekers say the church is insensitive to their needs and 37 percent say that the church is intolerant of them (meaning not their ideas or lifestyle choices but the people themselves!)

An explosion of new apostolic Christianity may burst some current wineskins just as the early Christian movement grew beyond the structures and strictures of first-century Judaism. New leadership is essential to reverse the current drift of the church into cultural and spiritual marginalization.

A mission versus maintenance tension. A final parallel between the two eras will bridge our discussion back to the leadership issue. The Jewish religious establishment that Jesus and his followers confronted was geared more toward maintenance than mission. The same can be said for many congregations in North America today. A maintenance approach to ministry focuses on programs for club members and maintaining the institution, with energy devoted to scheduling, budgeting, and other administrative deliberations affecting the life of the organization. A missional approach to ministry defines effectiveness in terms of changed lives as a result of prosecuting a proactive ministry agenda targeting people and their life issues and concerns.

Jesus did battle with a religious tradition that was intent on reliving the past. Tradition had evolved into a traditionalism that insulated Judaism from its mission field. Its leaders were more concerned about proper observance of rituals and practices than about the people who needed to discover God. Consequently, God was also postured to those outside the faith as a relic from bygone glory days. He was also represented as a stern taskmaster for those who could measure up, be accepted by him, and serve him.

The ministry of Christ challenged this perspective at every point (more about this in the next chapter). His ongoing criticism of first-century Judaism reached its white-hot zenith with the cleansing of the Temple during Passion Week and his final public "woes" delivered to the scribes and Pharisees. Jesus countered a maintenance attitude with teaching about a God who had a better future in mind for his people. He addressed real-life issues and went in search of people rather than waiting for them to come to him. He painted the picture of God as a reckless sower and a pining father. He insisted that his followers adopt his approach by proactively sharing their new found life, not fearing to target people whose life practices and values were very different from their own.

The North American church faces the same dilemma in terms of the tension between maintenance and mission. Unfortunately, many congregations have ceased to function with a missional agenda. They cling to the past. Each week they seek to provide a nostalgic experience for club members that is unintelligible to those who are not part of the church culture. Practices and programs have been elevated beyond the status of tradition to a traditionalism that is idolatrous. Mission to the world of unbelievers has yielded to an inward focus that insulates the congregation from the very people Jesus died for.

At this pivotal moment in history, God has orchestrated significant spiritual similarities akin to the birth century of Christianity. The book of Acts records the success of the Spirit of Christ in raising up apostolic leaders who eventually embraced God's mission of redemption as their ministry agenda. Leadership is once again needed that resembles leadership of the apostolic era—if we expect to see results similar to what they witnessed.

We must realize that the future of the church is up for grabs. The church will either become increasingly marginalized as a real player in shaping American culture or a renewal of biblical and Reformation proportions will reenergize the Christian community to embrace God's redemptive agenda. Leadership will make the choice. The direction that church leaders take in the next few years will shape not only the practice of Christian ministry but the character of the church's missional expression into the beginning of the third Christian millennium.

Prevailing Leadership Options

This volume argues that the emergence of new apostolic leadership will be necessary to lead the church into renewal. This new leadership model stands in contrast to the prevailing options from which church leaders currently choose. Some of these models have been more characteristic of church leaders during certain periods of history and in certain denominational cultures. None is mutually exclusive; in other words, a church leader may adopt more than one as an operating guide.

The Leader as Holy Person/Priest

. Most religious traditions set aside people who learn the rituals of the belief system. This knowledge qualitatively separates its possessors from the common adherents of the religious practice. In Jesus' day the Pharisees' knowledge of the law's demands set them apart from the ordinary Jewish worshiper. In the Christian tradition this basis for leadership gained ascendancy with the rise of the sacerdotal priesthood in the second and third centuries. An entire ecclesiastical system developed around this paradigm of church leadership.

The Leader as Wordsmith/Educator

The sixteenth-century revival of the study of antiquities and the rise of the modern university system found its religious counterpart in the Reformation. Luther and Calvin signaled a focus on textual authority and redefined the church leader's role as resident scholar in biblical studies. A heavy emphasis on preaching and teaching replaced the ceremonial focus of the Roman Catholic priesthood. Educational credentials and skills in oral communication became increasingly valued within denominational traditions heavily influenced by the Reformers. Leadership centered around the pulpit.

The Leader as Chaplain/Parish Minister

This model of leadership draws heavily on biblical motifs of shepherding. Within assigned geographical or denominational jurisdiction, the church leader operates as curator of souls among the flock. This model reached its fullest expression in the development of the state-church concept. People were born into the care of the church and shepherded throughout life, along with family members and others belonging to that same parish. Even in nonhierarchical or free church traditions this paradigm of ministry has remained formative.

The Leader as Professional Minister/Executive

With the rise of organizations in the twentieth century and the culture it created, a corresponding model for church leaders emerged: the minister as professional. This type of church leader marshals and manages resources in directing the church's ministry program and staff. Managerial expertise positions the leader for greater effectiveness. This set of management micro-skills becomes critical in leading larger congregations. Ministry expressed in the office is valued as well as performance in the pulpit.

The Emerging Apostolic Leader

The emerging model of leadership for the church of the future is one based on an apostolic style of leadership. It bears resemblance to the leadership of the first-century church in the following characteristics.

Visionary. Early church leaders gave their lives in pursuit of a compelling vision of the kingdom of God that Jesus shared with them. Modern church leaders who take seriously the Great Commission vision are captured by the prospect of a better future. They understand how to cultivate and to cast vision. Not only do they possess a personal vision that grips them, they know how to bring others on board with them to work for its realization. Such leaders realize that leading their congregations to do business as usual will not qualify as obedience to the Lord.

Missional. The New Testament reveals early Christian leaders making decisions and changing behaviors for the sake of the Great Mission (Acts 1:8). The Jerusalem Council in Acts 15 and the spread of the gospel to the Samaritans in Acts 8 and to the Gentiles in Acts 10 serve as prominent examples. Today's apostolic leaders are freshly challenging the church to evaluate its attitudes and activities in light of Jesus' last command before returning to the Father. These paradigm pioneers are practicing an intentionality in their ministries that shows up in kingdom expansion. They courageously refuse to let their congregations settle for maintenance ministry.

Empowering. As the number of early believers multiplied, the apostles made a strategic decision. They opted to share the ministry with others outside their immediate leadership circle (Acts 6:1-6). This risky move paid off. The church ministry entered a new era of expansion (Acts 6:7). The writings of the apostolic era indicate that the number of leadership assignments increased (Ephesians 4:11 and 1 Timothy 3:1-13, for instance). Effective church leaders today understand that the strategic way to leverage their ministry efforts is to empower others to minister. They devise systems to assist church members in discovering and developing ministry employment opportunities. They release the ministry from being bottlenecked in the hands of a few "professionals."

Team oriented and reproducing. Jesus had his Twelve. The early Jerusalem church was led by a senior team including some trained by the Master. Paul developed his Timothy, Luke, Silas, Barnabas, John Mark, and Titus. The apostle practiced team leadership and trained people to reproduce local leadership teams ("And the things you have heard me say . . . entrust to reliable men who will also be qualified to teach others," 2 Timothy 2:2 NIV).

New apostolic leaders practice and reproduce a leadership that is plural in its essence and expression. This new model moves beyond the CEO approach with its attendant tensions and trappings. Apostolic leaders of the future will make leadership development a priority of their ministry. They will know how to recruit and coach others into leadership excellence. Their legacy will be the quality of leaders they leave behind.

Entrepreneurial. The early church leaders were entrepreneurs in the classic sense of this word (those who organize, manage, and assume risk for a venture). They assumed stewardship of the Christian movement under the leadership of the Holy Spirit, who is the ultimate Entrepreneur. The apostles cooperated with the Spirit to rapidly expand their market. They knew how to connect the gospel with their culture. This did not present a challenge to them for several reasons. The founder of the movement had spent the first part of his adult life as a small business owner. He was immersed in the culture of his day. His recruitment practice reflected this bias. He called people out in order to send them back in. Apostolic-era leadership was indigenous. Preparation for leadership did not involve a credentialing regimen that removed emerging leadership from real life settings.

Emerging apostolic leaders take their cues from cultural exegesis in addition to their biblical insights. They take full advantage of opportunities for sharing the gospel in ways that unchurched people find appealing. This approach will involve far more ministry outside church walls. It necessitates a shift in thinking that begins to look for ways God is at work in the world, not just for what he is doing in the church. Rather than dreaming up church programs and then trying to attract people to them, apostolic leaders begin with their insights into people's needs and then design ministry efforts to meet them where they are.

Kingdom-conscious. The early church struggled with getting this one right. Early believers had to overcome a religious background informed by Judaism's exclusivism. Explosive growth occurred once they understood that the gospel was for everyone and God could be served in new ways. The leaders focused on reaching people in obedience to Christ, not on developing an institution. Not until old sacerdotal values reasserted themselves among leaders in the second and third centuries did kingdom concerns give way to institutional church concerns.

Today's new apostolic leaders are determined to prosecute a kingdom agenda for God's people. They are determined to follow Christ out into the world where they can dispel some darkness with his light. They join ranks with other believers to put Christianity into action in their communities. Those who can move beyond the constraints of "churchianity" discover an explosion of kingdom growth waiting to occur.

What would be the impact of a reemergence of apostolic-quality leadership? Key effects would include:

1. A reemphasis on the spiritual dimensions of leadership.

2. New leadership practices that are more ecclesial, that is, plural in nature, team-oriented in expression, and based on giftedness and call.

3. Redefinition of ministry benchmarks, moving from church growth concerns to issues of missional effectiveness.

4. A return of the work of God to the people of God, with the doctrine of the priesthood of all believers serving as a theological paradigm for renewal.

5. A church *in* the world rather than sociologically cocooned *from* it.

6. Urban and regional evangelism strategies that involve alliances among Christian groups and churches of diverse denominational backgrounds.

Where are we going to find leaders like this? The good news is, God is already raising them up. The bad news is, current methodologies for training church leaders do not provide adequate development of skills to meet apostolic leadership criteria. Leadership development has largely been done through the prevailing church culture, academic institutions such as Bible colleges and seminaries, and denominational efforts which have largely been program-driven, not vision-driven. These training entities have been informed in their efforts by a variety of past and current leadership models that no longer prove adequate.

There is better news. God never calls people to tasks he does not plan to resource. Early training for apostolic leadership has been emerging. It has largely come outside the traditional and formal credentialing pipeline of most denominational and academic systems. The source of this training has included new tribe pastors (effective pastors of new paradigm churches), several parachurch organizations, consultants, and the business culture. The last source has been valued for two reasons: its ability to exegete the culture and its development of leadership materials.

There is better news yet. The next strategy for equipping church leaders for a new apostolic era has already been formulated. The new process for leadership development will occur through peer mentoring that takes place in intentional learning communities.

Now, however, we are getting slightly ahead of ourselves. Before looking at this new paradigm for leadership development, we need to understand fully the impact of and context for apostolic leadership. To do that we have to return to God's design for his church.

2.

BACK TO THE FUTURE: APOSTOLIC CHURCHES

What drives the agendas of today's church leaders? Is it the Great Commission? Or is it a variety of other issues? Pastoral career concerns? Lust for power? Perpetuating the status quo? Providing hospice care for terminal churches? Restructuring the machinery? Raising money to meet budget or retire debt?

Leadership for a new apostolic era has a distinctive character to it. It is captured by and reflects the heart of God. Apostolic leadership seeks to partner with God in his redemptive mission in the world. Leaders of this ilk commit themselves to an agenda bent on transforming the world. This revolution begins with a different way of thinking and doing church. This chapter proposes a theological paradigm for renewal, providing clear biblical authority to fuel the emergence of apostolic congregations.

Refuge Versus Mission

The North American church faces a critical decision. The decision is about what agenda the church will pursue. The choice is clear. The options are two: thinking and doing church as *refuge* or thinking and doing church as *mission.* Leadership will make the choice.

The use of the word "refuge" in this context has a different connotation than usual. Obviously the church is a place of sanctuary, a place for respite. This notion, however, has been carried to extreme by many congregations. For purposes of our discussion, a refuge paradigm signals an approach to church that is characterized by a "let's hunker down and wait for the storm to blow over" mentality. Refuge congregations practice a lot of denial. They try to hang onto or even to recreate the past. They insulate themselves against the world around them, which they view as hostile and threatening to their survival. The future is viewed with fear. Outreach is mostly a matter of trying to keep the children in the faith or welcoming the newcomer out of the cold who already has the faith and has moved into the community. Activities are primarily geared to, operated with, and enjoyed by club members. The focus is obviously inward.

A mission mentality, on the other hand, is turned outward in its thinking and in its agenda. Churches operating with this paradigm seek cultural relevance and involvement. They not only risk involvement with the world, they strategize for it. Convinced that the harvest is ripe, these congregations search for ways to reach beyond the citadel and fortress of church real estate and programming. They measure their effectiveness through the number of transformed lives that enter into their community of faith from nonchurched or underchurched backgrounds. The church as mission faces the future with confidence and hope because it believes God is calling to his people from the better future he is preparing for them.

The original apostolic era posed the same options for God's people. The early leaders of the Christian movement came out of a first-century Judaism dominated by the Pharisees. This sect had perfected refuge religion. Pharisaism had its roots in a noble concern. Its heritage can be traced back to a spiritual movement that emerged in post-exilic times. The driving issue was how to preserve and pass down Jewish faith and values in pagan surroundings. A call to personal righteousness was seen as a remedy to the nation's ills. But the movement took a wrong turn. Refuge won out over mission.

By the time of Christ, the spiritual renewal movement that birthed Pharisaism had developed into a rigid sectarian religious party. The Pharisees had constructed a subculture that insulated them from "contamination" by the unclean world (which included most of their fellow citizens). Their fastidious attention to ritual cleansings is well documented. When they travelled from town to town, they stayed only with other Pharisees. Their social life revolved around sect members. They practiced a come-and-get-it evangelism strategy which forced people to jump through multiple cultural hoops before they could even be considered for club membership. The Pharisees' pursuit of personal righteousness had taken a social tack. Their well-known fixation with keeping Sabbath law grew out of a theological conviction that predicated the advent of the Messianic Age on getting enough people to satisfy the law's demands. In other words, if they could get enough people to act right, they could usher in the Kingdom of God. Thus proper adherence to Sabbath observances became a litmus test for true conformity to the faith. Meanwhile the ordinary and common Jews (dubbed "sinners" by the Pharisees) felt increasingly unable to meet God's demands as mediated by these ruling religious authorities. The aloofness and disdain of the Pharisees for those outside their group earned for them the reputation of being judgmental, self-righteous hypocrites.

Does any of this sound familiar? It should. Contemporary North American evangelicalism is headed down the same path. Our reaction to an increasingly hostile environment has been to substitute a moral social agenda for real evangelism and to burn, rather than build, bridges to the culture. The public persona of many who claim to speak for the church puts the unchurched off. Judgmental attitudes and self-righteousness stiff-arm the very people Jesus came to embrace. Many contemporary church leaders would decry any comparison to the Pharisees. After all, were not they Jesus' enemies? Yes, indeed.

Jesus grew up listening to the Pharisees' message. They controlled the synagogues where almost all religious instruction took place in first-century Judaism. The Temple, under control of the Sadducees, performed a mostly ritual and symbolic function. Imagine the frustration that grew inside of Jesus as he heard the Pharisees' message of legalism and exclusivism. This focus painted a wrong portrait of his Father. We might suspect that part of his conversations in his boyhood Temple visit recorded in Luke 2 addressed these themes. Who knows what exchanges Jesus may have had with the local teachers in Nazareth!

The Lord left no doubt during his public ministry concerning his views of the Pharisees. Nothing pushed his hot buttons like their attitudes. He excoriated their hypocrisy, ridiculed their focus, and warned their potential devotees against the sterility of their religion. His last public utterances contained his famous "woes" to the Pharisees and scribes. Jesus' notions of the kingdom of God ran directly counter to the prevailing religious teaching imbibed by the population from the Pharisees. He described an inclusive God of grace and love. Against the Pharisees' come-and-get-it mentality, he commissioned his followers to "go, get 'em." Rather than avoiding "sinners" as the Pharisees did, Jesus actively sought them out. The Father he portrayed was on a redemptive mission in the world.

The book of Acts records the successful struggle of the first-century apostolic leaders to overcome their own background in Pharisaic Judaism. They had grown up hearing what Jesus had heard. To move from a refuge to a mission paradigm required a major shift in their thinking. The apostles were aided in redrawing their mind maps by the miraculous intervention and coaching of the Holy Spirit. Because they adopted the mission model, the Christian movement spread and thrived. Following the lead of Jesus' Spirit, they engaged unbelievers rather than avoiding them. They crossed cultural, religious, political, and geographical boundaries in pursuit of their mission. They caught the heart of God for all people.

A new apostolic era will require the church to recapture the heart of God for his world. Leadership will again play a pivotal role in making the choice between a refuge agenda and a mission agenda. This is why the emergence of apostolic leadership is so crucial. Authentic renewal will come to the North American church when God's people are led to accept their commission to live on mission with him in the world.

A Theology for Renewal

Leaders for a new apostolic era will lead from a solid theological base, following the example of first-century Christian leaders. We need a theological paradigm to support a missional revolution. The Bible provides one: the doctrine of the priesthood of all believers. The biblical concept of the universal priesthood of believers offers the most corrective theology for challenging the contemporary North American church to choose mission over refuge.

The recurrence of this believer-priest theme in scripture signals that it is forever on God's mind. The initial expression of the doctrine occurs on a significant occasion. After their escape from slavery in Egypt, the people of God came to Sinai. For Moses the event completed the fulfillment of Yahweh's promise, which was given to him when he was commissioned as the leader of the enslaved nation. God had assured Moses that a free Israel would worship him on the mountain of the burning bush (see Exodus 3:12). With eager anticipation Moses ascended the mountain to meet with Yahweh.

> Then Moses went up to God, and the LORD called to him from the mountain and said, "This is what you are to say to the house of Jacob and what you are to tell the people of Israel: 'You yourselves have seen what I did to Egypt, and how I carried you on eagles' wings and brought you to myself. Now if you obey me fully and keep my covenant, then out of all nations you will be my treasured possession. Although the whole earth is mine, you will be for me a kingdom of priests and a holy nation.' These are the words you are to speak to the Israelites." (Exodus 19:3-6 NIV)

In this covenant proposal God designated Israel as a "kingdom of priests" among all peoples of the world. Israel's commission from Yahweh involved all the people, not just a select few, as priests. What they learned about him as they served him was to be shared with others. However, Israel failed to fulfill its obligation to "priest" the world, despite God's repeated reminders throughout the Old Testament period.

Israel's failure did not alter God's plan to create a people on mission with him in the world. He shifted the commission to the new Israel, the church. The apostle Peter used both the idea and the language of Exodus 19 when he wrote to first-century believers.

> You also, like living stones, are being built into a spiritual house to be a holy priesthood, offering spiritual sacrifices acceptable to God through Jesus Christ . . . But you are a chosen people, a royal priesthood, a holy nation, a people belonging to God, that you may declare the praises of him who called you out of darkness into his wonderful light. (1 Peter 2:5,9 NIV)

The missional import of this passage cannot be overstated. God's creation of a new people is for the purpose of revealing himself to the rest of the world. The priests of God have a responsibility as a result of their relationship with him. A commission accompanies their call out from the kingdom of darkness into the kingdom of God.

A third explicit use of this commissioning language occurs in John's final book. The apostle began his message to the churches by reminding them of their relationship to God through Christ, who "has made us to be a kingdom and priests to serve his God and Father" (Revelation 1:6 NIV). Later, while describing a worship experience in heaven, the apostle hears the same missional refrain. The elders and creatures around the throne break into a song of praise to the Lamb.

> You are worthy to take the scroll and to open its seals, because you were slain, and with your blood you purchased men for God from

every tribe and language and people and nation. You have made them to be a kingdom and priests to serve our God, and they will reign on the earth. (Revelation 5:9-10 NIV)

This brief recital of biblical texts indicates the tenacious and eternal intention of God to create a people who join him on his redemptive mission in the world. Even the verb tenses of the passages reflect this truth. The Exodus record uses a future tense ("you *will be* for me a kingdom of priests") whereas Peter adopted the present tense to describe God's design for the church ("you *are* a royal priesthood"). Christians of any age always operate with this present tense understanding. In John's vision the tense of this theme shifts again. This time the text uses the aorist tense, reflecting a completed action ("you *have made* them to be a kingdom and priests"). The message is clear. What God starts, he finishes. His eternal purpose is that his people live missionally, serving as his representatives, his "priests."

This doctrine carries enormous implications about the way God intends for us to "do" church. Universal priesthood, courageously practiced, would bring renewal to the church by reestablishing its missional integrity. Signs of missional vitality powered by the priesthood of all believers would include:

- vibrant worship characterized by praise. Christian priests offer up spiritual sacrifices in the praise of him who has called them out of darkness.
- a multi-faceted expression of ministry reflecting the spiritual giftedness of believers. The call and gifts are inseparable. God's priests are equipped to fulfill the commission of brokering him to the world in ways that reflect their unique passions, gifts, and personality.
- an infrastructure of caring and discipling that fosters mutual accountability among believers for spiritual formation. Believers also priest one another by bearing one another's burdens and coaching each other to spiritual growth.

• a redirection of church resources and energy to engage the world beyond the walls of church property and programming. The bulk of Christian priests' time and energy is spent in nonchurch arenas. With every believer on mission, every life venue becomes a ministry opportunity.

Four Paradigm Shifts

This type of renewal is the antidote for sterile and innocuous Christianity. Nothing less will reverse the slide toward marginalization of the North American church. Revitalization of mission will come only if apostolic leadership boldly challenges the church to undergo four crucial paradigm shifts.

Shift 1: From Top-down to Flat Line

The church needs to shift from top-down to flat line in terms of who is authorized and expected to be engaged in ministry. The presenting question for consideration in this paradigm shift is, *Who is empowered for what?* Typical church thinking views the ministry as clergy-driven and clergy-dominated, the province of those credentialed to represent God. The laity serves mostly by providing a resource pool of time, energy, and money to generate and operate the clergy's program.

Missional churches empower God's people for genuine ministry. They do not just invite them to come alongside the "professionals" as their helpers. Providing venues and strategies for Christians to discover their spiritual gifts and passion is just the beginning of ministry empowerment. Church organizations and the process of recruitment must be reengineered in order to move from a program-based to a gifts-based approach.

Returning the work of God to the people of God would release a revolution of apostolic proportions. What would this mean for the clergy? In a church setting that gives full expression to Christian priesthood crucial functions still remain for clergy. Their responsibilities focus mainly on being vision casters, equippers, and coaches to release people into effective ministry.

The codependent relationships between many clergy and their congregations can make this shift difficult to accomplish. Unfortunately the failure to address this challenge threatens the health and missional effectiveness of the church. Besides creating burnout, family problems, and a whole host of other disorders, the current clergy-killing church culture actually prevents ministry from expanding. One wonders what might happen if clergy financial support were based on the effectiveness of church members' ministry rather than on the clergy's personal ministry performance or ability to captivate a large enough group of believers to afford them a stipendiary income.

Shift 2: From Inside to Inside-out

Congregations must also shift from inside to inside-out. The question begging attention here is *Where is the front line?* in terms of kingdom expansion. Typical church thinking declares the front to be church property and programs. The church's resources of time, energy, attention, and worry focus on institutional and organizational efforts, within the walls of the church building, designed to keep the church going. The trouble is that the number of people in this culture exposed to or even intrigued by church programming has plateaued at best.

A mission-driven church realizes that the front line of spiritual battle, where the kingdoms of light and darkness collide, is in the home, the school, the office, the health club, civic organizations, the relational neighborhoods, and wherever it is that Christian priests find themselves primarily engaged. The ministry venues for believer-priests are desks, phones, cyberspace, restaurant tables, ballpark bleachers, and den sofas. This theological perspective holds to the view that it makes sense for God to place his people where they can make a difference in the world that does not know him yet.

When the front becomes confused in the thinking of Christians, the church does strange things. It takes people off the front lines and monasticizes them through too many church activities and responsibilities. When the front is correctly identified, the church does courageous things. It streamlines its programs and organization so Christian priests can spend more time "priesting" their families, each other, and the world.

Shift 3: From Outside to Outside-in

The church must shift from outside to outside-in. The question that helps us to understand this paradigm shift is *Are we operating with the mission in mind?* Put another way, is the church in touch with the culture enough to know how to respond effectively? Also, is there a willingness to let those on the outside come in? The typical approach takes an attitude of "come and get it." This perspective assumes that people know what they need, they know the church has it, and they are willing to come onto church turf to receive it. These assumptions need challenging when the church borders on being as sociologically insulated as was first-century Pharisaic Judaism.

Missional church ministry flows out of an attitude and philosophy that says, "we will meet you where you are." By identifying, understanding, and meeting the needs of unchurched people, believers live up to their calling to proclaim God's praises for the difference he has made in their lives. Adopting this theological paradigm and ministry philosophy means that the church does not require that people get their act together before coming to God. The "club members only" mentality that exists in many congregations will need to be overcome. Christian consumerism will come under the knife. Worship experiences will be more culturally relevant as well as spiritually energized because of a newfound sense of mission and an awe of what God is up to in the world. Authentic expressions of love and grace will replace hypocritical attitudes of judgment and retreat from people who do not share Christian values.

Shift 4: From the Edge to the Center

A final shift must be made in order for God's people to experience missional living. The church must move God from the edge to the center. Another question helps to focus this issue: *Where are we looking for God to be at work?* Standard thinking among Christians allows religious activity to occupy the fringes as only one among many life compartments. This sacred/secular dichotomy fosters a Christianity that presumes evangelism and discipleship are unrelated to each other and optional concerns for the typical believer. This thinking imprisons God to the confines of religious matters. Further, God is seen as operating most comfortably within the church, with the world eluding and baffling him while going its own way.

Missional thinking of a new apostolic era recognizes that God is at work in the world, calling Christians out to play. God views the world as a field "white unto harvest." Serving the Lord of harvest gives direction and meaning to all life's activities for the believer-priest. A mission-driven church provides encouragement and support for Christians who find their calling outside the church, who want to make a difference in the world beyond the church for Christ's sake. Christian commitment is not measured by participation in church activities.

These foundational shifts will not occur without new leadership. However, merely exposing church leaders to new ideas or up-to-date methodologies will not be enough to pull off the revolution that must occur. New thinking and, just as significantly, new behavior, must replace current leadership attitudes and practices. Nothing less will be able to guide the church into a new apostolic era.

Where will we get the leaders we need? Most likely they are already available. It would be just like God to have anticipated the need. How will they develop the skills and stamina they need to effect a revolution? That is an intriguing question. The answer does not lie in traditional training approaches. A new model for leadership development must arise.

It already has. It is called the learning community.

3.

THE CASE FOR THE LEARNING COMMUNITY

A leadership revolution will require a learning revolution. The competencies required of apostolic leaders outstrip the production capability of current academic training processes. In this chapter we will take a look at what these competencies are and why traditional educational approaches are inadequate to develop them. We will identify some learning and unlearning challenges facing apostolic leaders. Finally we will suggest an alternative leadership development model: the learning community.

Special Leadership Competencies

In addition to its unique character and call, apostolic leadership is also distinguished by its competencies. The following list of personal competencies will characterize effective twenty-first-century leadership.

Vision. This attribute is the ability to cultivate and communicate a compelling, preferred future that motivates and measures the missional expression of the leader and the church. Apostolic leadership cannot develop without this powerful personal vision. It enables the leader to navigate from a secure internal guidance system. The contemporary apostolic leader has to understand what his call is and what he has answered the call to do.

Values/Spiritual Formation. Vision is the seed. Values are the soil. Values will either support and nurture the growth of a vision or starve its development. This is why vision-value alignment is critical for the leader. The apostolic leader must pay close attention to his heart, the battleground for values clarification. Discernment and intentionality are required in order to develop life around priority pursuits that undergird vision and integrate life experiences with the goal of maintaining spiritual vitality.

Intuition. This attribute captures the ability of the leader to engage information at a level that is fundamentally different from logical cognition, to gather decision-making data from hunches and feelings that extend beyond surface analysis. Few academic institutions offer courses on developing intuition, yet this skill will grow increasingly important for leadership effectiveness during white-water change. Leaders will need to feel and to hunch their way through new situations that present themselves from outside the parameters of the typical. This skill is not guessing, but it calls into play the full experience of the leader in dealing with issues he has not encountered quite like this before. The prayer life of the church leader certainly comes into play here, along with issues of timing and discernment. Kingdom enterprise takes the leader and congregation into dimensions that extend beyond the rational. Congregational and individual behaviors often reflect subrational forces that intuitive leaders are more apt to anticipate and to grasp.

Risk Taking. This is the ability to know when and why to take risks. Christian leaders in pivotal times throughout church history have taken risks that have paid off in advancing God's mission. Leaders who refuse to take risks in today's climate will cease to be leaders. Most churches, afraid to risk failure, fail to enjoy success. Missional leaders and congregations simply cannot advance without risk. Love implies risk. We are called to love.

Systems Thinking. This competency allows the leader to understand the systemic impact of variables in both diagnosing problems and prescribing solutions or courses of action. An effective church leader knows, "If I do this, then this will impact these other elements in the system." Another benefit of systems thinking is the ability of the leader to do analytical thinking that extends beyond presenting symptoms to identifying and treating root causes.

Opportunity Making/Opportunity Taking. The apostolic leader knows how to create opportunity with a significant shift toward a proactive ministry posture. This contrasts sharply with the maintenance leader who is trained and conditioned by the existing church culture to deal with events and people as they appear on the program calendar or come through the door. Entrepreneurial leaders begin with human needs that exist apart from organizational concerns. Then they lead their churches to design ministry efforts and allocate resources to deliver assistance in Jesus' name. Twenty-first-century apostolic leaders and churches will create new markets for the gospel. Through value-added approaches to ministry, they will enable people to discover Christ while getting help for their lives.

Trust. One of the primary leadership strategies that recaptures a significant element of the New Testament leadership dynamic is the development of teamwork. Trust is the currency of teams. Trust can be described as the willingness to rely on others through appropriate vulnerability. This is a tough competency to develop because it goes against natural, self-protecting tendencies. Team members who trust other team players are empowered to do their best without using energy protecting their turf or flank. This element proves extremely important for empowering lay ministry. Creating an atmosphere of trust depends mostly on the leader, who often has to take the first step in developing trust by demonstrating trust.

Coaching/Developing Support. Apostolic leaders know both how to serve as coaches to their own leadership teams and how to seek out support for their own efforts. They support and coach others through sharing assignments, offering observations, giving appropriate directions, providing accountability, and celebrating achievement. These same leaders have rejected a Lone Ranger mentality, choosing instead to invite the support of others. These leaders develop support for more than ministry goals. They also generate support for their personal lives and spiritual needs.

Take another look at the preceding list. These are crucial leadership competencies. They are also scarce. Why? Part of the reason lies in the fact that these skills and competencies are not learned in an academic or seminar setting, our traditional ways of preparing church leaders. The seminarian is credentialed through mastery of academic topics: history, theology, and such. The assumption that a seminary graduate is "prepared" by such antiquated training foci to lead churches needs to be more than challenged. Many church leaders, feeling this preparation gap, have employed survival tactics, such as taking Doctor of Ministry studies, reading voraciously, and becoming seminar junkies. Even these attempts to stay prepared have not been able to keep pace with learning demands.

Church leaders are not alone in this struggle to maintain preparedness. Leaders in every facet of our culture are confronting these same challenges. They are handicapped by the inherent limits of typical learning processes. This does not mean that we should throw out all the ways we have been taught. We need, instead, to realize that most of the learning that we have done in formal classrooms, from childhood on, has the following limiting factors.

Cognitive-Targeted. Most of our education has targeted our cognition. We could not develop without cognitive learning, but we certainly need to know much that falls outside the usual scope of cognitive development. In our congregations we have often assumed that if people had adequate information they would develop into mature Christians. We know, however, that many things about God transcend the rational and do not yield to cognitive investigation alone. Apostolic leadership is not developed primarily through exposure to new information.

Linear. We have been instructed in linear thinking: A, then B, then C. This is cause-and-effect thinking. The world, however, does not behave linearly. Life is not lived linearly but usually on simultaneous layers. When we learn, we do not construct knowledge one piece at a time. We sometimes suddenly capture a whole field of understanding at breakthrough moments. We have to visit and revisit material in order to learn it. We have to explore again at different levels. We layer learning. In our leadership training we have often ignored these learning dynamics. We need to understand that learning is 360 degrees.

Prescriptive. Obviously early learning involves prescription of necessity. People are well served to be moved to principle-driven learning as soon as possible. The first generation of church growth materials, for example, were heavily prescriptive. Church leaders often took home prescriptions from seminars for their churches that were not contextualized, usually against the warnings of the seminar presenters. Often the attempt to introduce these learnings into the congregation back home created tension. In some cases the only change that took place was the change of address for the seminar participant! Analytical thinking and reflection must distill out principles that can be contextualized and implemented.

Parochial/Perspective Bound. Most of the teaching we have been exposed to has been parochial or perspective-bound in its view of the truth. Limited perspective is unavoidable and is one of the challenges of any learning situation, including the development of leaders. Some people tend to globalize and assert their own experiences. They believe everyone's experience has been or should be the same as theirs. Until this parochial perspective is transcended, learning will be missed.

Isolated. Much of our learning model in this culture assumes an individual consumer working privately, isolated from other learners. We work on assignments by ourselves throughout our educational pursuits. This model certainly characterizes seminary training even though students are preparing to enter a ministry that will be done most effectively in teams. Individual learning is still a dominant dynamic in many congregations. No debriefing is provided for gleaning what individual Christians are learning about life. Leadership does not arise just by amassing experience, but is developed by intentional reflection on that experience. Reflection proves most insightful when it is guided, not done in isolation.

Primarily Didactic. The process of our learning has primarily involved the transfer of information from teacher to pupil. We have been taught to glean information from authorities, to learn something from someone who can pass it down to us. The church culture certainly has heavy investment in this learning model. Often clergy are regarded as the instructors in spiritual matters. This model of ministry, which became dominant in Protestant churches as Reformation leaders clung to the university system, still dominates the church culture and academic training for ministry. The focus is on teaching rather than learning.

This discussion on changing paradigms of learning is carried forward in chapter twelve. There the specific focus is on implications for seminary education.

New learning challenges for leaders do not stop inside the classroom. Some well-entrenched assumptions and behaviors that have long held reign in the "real world" are also biting the dust. These developments add to the learning challenges of leaders. These challenges can be summed up in the following three statements:

1. Leaders can no longer rely on control and planning for effectiveness. The new requirement for leadership is to be prepared to meet any challenge.

Old paradigm organizations that are hierarchical relied largely on control to maintain corporate effectiveness. The top managers supervised middle management, who supervised others, and so on. Through supervisory control, propped up by information and access to budgets, the management ran the company. Management got their game plan together through planning. Budget planning, calendar planning, and marketing and sales strategy planning used to be done by departments. Strategic planning attempted to integrate these and anticipate the future challenges to the corporation.

Translated into the church setting, the old paradigm church culture is hierarchical both in terms of decision-making and ministry empowerment. Those credentialed with information (in the form of special theological training) control the ministry. Those vested with budgets sometimes control the decision-making. Church program life is often controlled by calendar and denominational emphases. This type of church culture will not foster an environment for learning that will support the renewal needed for the American church to avoid marginalization in our culture.

Preparedness is the new paradigm. Leaders must be prepared to meet any challenge. They do not have three to five years to address the issues that present themselves. When you go to a hospital emergency room, you expect them to be prepared to meet any challenge. When operating from a preparedness paradigm, the leader positions himself and his congregation to be ready for the intervention of God and to follow him when it comes.

You may respond to this with the question, "How can I anticipate everything that is going to come our way?" The answer is, you cannot. Not by yourself.

2. Success is now dependent upon our ability to create new knowledge together with colleagues.

No one can learn fast enough alone anymore. What needs to be learned is too huge a body of knowledge for any one person to master. This is true in the church world. Will you learn everything about the five generations of Americans now living above ground? Or will you focus on worship? What legal issues, if left untended, expose your church to risk? On and on goes the list of special bodies of information that you could master.

But the learning challenge extends beyond grasping what is out there to learn. Much of what we need to know has not been thought up yet. It is not out there for us to access, at least not in predigested and prepackaged forms. What we need to know is out there in other people who are facing similar situations. They may have the one piece that completes the puzzle for us. This is called peer mentoring, and it is the future of learning.

3. Mastery of the knowledge-building process is the competitive capital for twenty-first-century leadership success.

Understanding how to construct knowledge is an essential micro-skill set for apostolic leaders. Preparedness is hardly something read in a book or picked up from the travelling seminar expert. The kind of knowledge required for preparedness must draw on experience. However, no single leader can amass enough personal experience to prepare for contemporary challenges. Leadership challenges are too diverse and come too quickly for a single experiential base to be an adequate source for insight. The implications for this are two-fold: we must learn from a wider experiential base than our own, and we must learn how to create new knowledge together with other leaders who face similar challenges. This ability to create new knowledge will be a key piece of intellectual capital for effective leaders in the twenty-first century.

The Learning Community Paradigm

Help is on the way. A new learning paradigm is emerging for leaders: the learning community. One definition of a learning community reads like this: *A group of colleagues who come together in a spirit of mutual respect, authenticity, learning, and shared responsibility to continually explore and articulate an expanding awareness and base of knowledge. The process of learning community includes inquiring about each other's assumptions and biases, experimenting, risking, and openly assessing the results.*[1]

Does this sound familiar? Reflect again on the apostolic era. With the whole world to save, Jesus decided to create a learning community. He called a group together to share a journey and to learn from him the most incredible truths ever revealed to humanity. The apostles watched and listened as Jesus worked and taught. They debriefed together the experiences they shared. Jesus sent them out on mission and unpacked their experiences when they returned. Along the way he challenged their notions about what God was up to in the world.

The band of apostles maintained their learning community even after Jesus' departure. The ability of the group to shift operational and missional paradigms can be directly related to their new knowledge construction process. They kept learning. New experiences and challenges pushed their learning curve. They had no how-to books or experts. They had each other, their experiences, the Holy Spirit as a coach, and a commitment to take results seriously. Their learning path sharpened their vision, shaped their values, and changed the world.

We are on the threshold of a new apostolic era. The challenges leaders face are similar to those that confronted the first-century Christian leaders. Their method of learning can be instructive for us. Today's church leaders need to be part of a learning community.

In short, church leaders need to be forming and participating in learning clusters.

4

A New Leadership Development Model for Apostolic Leaders

The emergence of leadership for a new apostolic era will require new methods for development and training. The prevailing academic model cannot produce the kind of leadership that is now needed to release a biblically informed, spiritual revival of mission in order to prevent the church's marginalization in this culture. Renovating curriculum content and rewriting degree programs will not accomplish the needed leadership revolution. These efforts cannot address the inherent limitations of prevalent educational models that militate against the rise of effective leadership to face today's challenges. The entire delivery system for church leadership must be changed, not just the contents of the existing pipeline. The search is on for a new approach that has as its end result a new breed of leader in terms of call, character, and competence.

This chapter presents one process aimed at meeting these requirements. The process is an application of the learning community concept introduced in the last chapter. It is currently under implementation as part of the leadership development strategy for the South Carolina Baptist Convention (SCBC). This denominational entity includes nearly 1900 churches with about 730,000 members—about the same size as a mid-sized denomination in contemporary American Christianity. The congregations employ approximately 2500 pastors and full-time staff members. Several hundred more leaders serve staff positions in part-time and bivocational capacities. Thousands of lay leaders join with them to make up the leadership corps in Southern Baptist churches in South Carolina. These churches reflect a profile that validates a widely held axiom about the growth status of American churches. The majority of these congregations are either plateaued or declining. Turning this situation around clearly presents a leadership challenge.

Faced with this situation and with the task of resourcing the multitude of church leaders in our state, we have developed what we call a *learning cluster model.* This approach attempts the development of apostolic leaders through the establishment of learning communities. The goal of this effort is to effect changed leadership behavior resulting in more missional churches that are prosecuting an intentional kingdom growth agenda.

The following overview of our learning cluster strategy provides an architectural blueprint of this plan. The discussion that follows unpacks this new leadership development process.

SCBC Leadership Development Strategy Involving Learning Clusters

Purpose: To develop a process for leadership development for pastors, staff, and key lay leaders that supplements academic and conference learning and captures experiential insights in an atmosphere of mutual encouragement.

A. Philosophical bases and core concerns
   1. The need for leadership training
   2. The isolation of church leaders and churches
   3. The debilitation of loneliness and feelings of insignificance
   4. The dynamic of small group support

    5. The issue of integration of information
    6. The value of plural leadership learning
    7. The vision of EKG (shorthand for "Empowering Kingdom Growth"—the stated vision of the South Carolina Baptist Convention)

B. Cluster components
    1. Size: four pastors or church staff leaders plus their leadership constellation
    2. Cluster affinities: size of church, philosophy of ministry, ministry agenda and situation, age, tenure and experience, location, and personality and temperament
    3. Duration: two years with annual covenant renewal
    4. Entry qualifications: attendance at a shared learning experience, covenant commitment to accountability and confidentiality, the willingness to produce a learning experience with others in the cluster, and covenant renewed annually
    5. Cluster calendar: six to eight meetings of cluster core quartet annually and semiannual or annual learning event coproduced for learning constellations of the four churches
    6. Cluster leadership: a facilitator, who is one of the quartet, is selected annually by the SCBC Leadership Director, has a separate covenant of expectations and benefits, and receives semiannual facilitator's training
    7. Recruitment: facilitator enlistment

C. Curriculum
    1. Two-day entry learning event structured by the SCBC Leadership Team
    2. First-year's curriculum revisits parts of the entry learning event
    3. Additional curriculum pieces designed and produced by SCBC Leadership Team
D. Cluster management
    1. Facilitators coached in recruitment strategies

   2. Semiannual facilitators' training
   3. Records of cluster activity maintained in SCBC Leadership Team office

E. Cost
   1. Entry events heavily subsidized by SCBC
   2. Facilitators' training provided as bonus to cluster leadership
   3. Curriculum production and distribution costs borne by SCBC
   4. Support for leadership constellation conferences produced by clusters

F. Distance learning possibilities
   1. Entry events
   2. New curriculum components
   3. Cluster constellation conference feeds
   4. Combination of satellite, compressed video, and CD-ROM delivery

G. Cluster time line
   1. Recruitment of facilitators at JOSHUA PROJECT (an intensive leadership development event produced by SCBC Leadership Team) in February
   2. Facilitator training in April
   3. Clusters recruited by June
   4. Clusters launched in August
   5. Facilitator training in December
   6. Constellation conferences in winter
   7. Facilitator training and cluster celebration in May
   8. Cluster covenant renewal in summer

Purpose

Several key words and phrases capture significant features of this leadership development model using cluster learning.

Process. Learning cannot be forced, but a process that facilitates learning can be implemented. The process approach recognizes the lifelong and ongoing nature of leadership development. The learning journey is the destination. Earning degrees or completing courses of study are not a part of this model.

Leadership development. The focus of this process model is not on acquisition of a set of facts or a body of knowledge. The goal is to develop leaders. If leaders are changed, then churches can be changed. God's apparent chosen method of calling his people to mission is through an intervention strategy that often involves leaders.

Pastors, staff, and key lay leaders. Our approach seeks to avoid the Lone Ranger approach to leadership practice. Many denominational and parachurch training efforts have almost exclusively targeted the pastor in hopes of impacting the church. This single-gatekeeper approach does not address a significant challenge to changing the vision or values of the congregation. At least the top echelon of leaders in the church have to share a common sense of purpose and direction. This is particularly true for churches who wish to prosecute a missional agenda. Our model involves congregational, lay leadership as well as clergy. Apostolic era leadership was plural in nature. New apostolic era churches will emerge only if lay leadership is on the same page as clergy.

Supplements conference and academic learning. As has been pointed out already, a huge gap exists between traditional training and field needs. There is little evidence that knowledge by itself changes behavior. Conference and academic learning exposes the leader to knowledge and helps to raise some agenda. However, changed leadership behavior will require a different learning process.

Captures experiential insights. Two ideas find expression here. First, the key part that experience plays in leadership development is given appropriate attention. Every leader is shaped by circumstances and challenges. The leader's experience base provides grist for the mill of leadership development. Second, experience alone does not always prove a great teacher unless insights can be gleaned from it. The learning cluster model creates intentional learning venues where guided debriefings of experience can occur. This approach often accelerates the leader's learning and development. Jesus understood this. He spent three years using this method of guided debriefing to prepare the apostolic leadership corps for the Christian movement. He quizzed the disciples on their understanding of his public teaching. He reviewed their own ministry efforts and helped them unpack their questions.

An atmosphere of mutual encouragement. The learning cluster model takes seriously the cry from pastors and church leaders that "we need each other," but acknowledges the special prerequisites for significant sharing to be facilitated. People do not open up readily in hostile or unprotected environments. Ask any church leader. He or she will tell you that church leaders as a group trust each other very little. One reason commonly given for this mistrust is competition. But if you dig very deep into church leaders' lives you will find a scar left by a fellow pastor or church leader who betrayed their relationship. The key to creating the kind of atmosphere conducive to sharing is establishing a covenant relationship between the members of the cluster.

Learning Cluster Architecture

Let us look at some specific design features of the learning cluster model. The outline that follows is a modified version of the one on pages 53-55. We begin by recounting the rationale or presenting needs that give rise to this approach.

A. Core Issues and Driving Concerns

1. The need for leadership training. The emergence of a new brand of leader is the greatest need the church has. Current product development and delivery systems are producing leaders that are increasingly market irrelevant.

2. The isolation of church leaders and congregations. Most church leaders and congregations assume they face unique challenges that no one else shares. They are not positioned to learn from what others are doing. Void of any new ideas or methodological insights, they continue doing the same thing they have done in their living memory. This withdrawal is a symptom of denial and poor self-esteem.

3. *The debilitation of loneliness and feelings of insignificance.* Pastors report that they battle loneliness and insignificance. This condition results directly from the isolation that church leaders and congregations feel. Church leaders lament having few, if any, vital and nurturing relationships. Most feel that since they do not serve a high profile church, no one pays any attention to their work, leaving them wondering about the value of their contribution and calling.

4. *The challenge of behavioral change for leaders.* Unless leaders act differently, nothing much will change in terms of churches becoming more missional. Leaders must cast a vision of a preferred future, coach their leadership, empower people for ministry, and proactively maintenance their personal lives. This is only the beginning of the list. Leaders raised in and trained for existing church-age ministry typically do not manifest these behavioral characteristics.

5. *The power of guided debriefings of ministry and life experiences.* Programs and processes most successful in changing behavior understand the importance of small group dynamics in supporting and coaching. People challenged by similar goals can bind together to support each other and hold each other accountable for growth. The key that unlocks the door to improvement is honest assessment of life experiences. This includes unpacking baggage picked up along the way.

6. *The value of same-page learning for multiple leadership levels in congregations.* The pastor, or even the pastor and staff together, cannot pull off the needed revolution in leadership. Any efforts at significant behavioral change toward greater missional intentionality will require the cooperation of at least the first key level of lay leadership in the congregation. Forging a coalition of leaders that can transition the church into a new apostolic era means,

at the very least, exposing lay leaders to the critical issues involved. The maxim "They kill the messenger" describes the welcome awaiting the inspired pastor or staff member returning home from the conference that has fired her imagination and renewed her vision. Greater efforts must be expended at getting the same information to the lay leaders through another gate, not forcing the pastor or staff leaders to be the messengers. Denominational leaders, by the way, can play a significant and helpful role in this regard. The cluster model approaches this through the venue of multi-congregational learning events.

7. The value of peer mentoring. The days are gone when enough expertise could be leveraged into ministry situations through traditional channels of seminars, books, tapes, and so forth. Church leaders are facing challenges that arise so quickly, and on such a broad scale, they must take responsibility for their own learning. However, they cannot learn enough or fast enough on their own. They need learning partners who are facing similar ministry challenges. This is the need for peer mentoring, the same dynamic which was at work in the first century. Asking cluster learners to pass their learning on to others in their cluster and congregation steepens their learning curves.

B. Learning Cluster Design and Process

1. Size. Four pastors or church leaders form the core of the cluster. Four is not an arbitrary number. If the cluster is comprised of only three members, the unexpected and unavoidable absence of one member would leave only a pair of learners at a cluster meeting. With only two present the group dynamic evaporates. On the other hand, if a cluster gets much larger than four, the amount of airtime available for each member rapidly diminishes. We do have some five-member clusters. A cluster probably should not exceed a maximum number of six. Beyond that size the learning dynamic shifts away from the mentoring intensity. Another consideration in limiting the size of the group relates to scheduling for the participants and for churches setting up multi-congregational events (called constellation conferences in our process). Cluster learning includes church leaders beyond the ministerial staff through these occasional constellation conferences. The cluster members determine whom they will include in this larger leadership constellation. The composition will vary from group to group. Candidates for consideration include spouses of cluster members, other church staff members, ministry leaders, worship leaders, deacons, elders, Bible study leaders, program leaders, mission organization leaders, committee leaders and members, informal leaders, and emerging leaders.

2. *Leadership.* A facilitator gives leadership to the cluster and serves as one of its members. In our case the leadership or facilitator pool comprises alumni of the JOSHUA PROJECT, an intensive five-day leadership development event we produce. We present this cluster learning opportunity as part of the JOSHUA PROJECT and ask those interested in convening a cluster to sign up for a facilitator training event where they will be coached in their role. The facilitator then enters into a covenant acknowledging leadership expectations (a copy of this covenant is included in the appendix at the end of the book).

3. *Cluster membership and entry requirements.* Cluster members are recruited by a facilitator on the basis of affinity and become eligible for cluster participation by attending a shared learning experience and by covenanting with other cluster members (a copy of the member covenant is also included in the appendix). Facilitators consider several affinities when recruiting their cluster. Obviously every cluster member does not possess each trait. These considerations simply guide facilitators in thinking through their cluster composition. Affinities for consideration include: ministry role, size of worshiping congregation, philosophy of ministry, ministry agenda and situation, age of church and leader, tenure and experience of leader, geographical location, and personality and temperament. Member covenants address accountability issues, confidentiality of group discussion, and the shared learning responsibilities of participants. The shared learning experience is pro-

duced by the SCBC on an annual basis. We call this the cluster launch conference. We cover the same basic material that the facilitators were exposed to at the JOSHUA PROJECT. This redundancy serves a double purpose. The facilitators have confidence about what they are inviting fellow learners to be a part of. In addition, the cluster launch conference provides a same-page learning experience to birth the group. All of the cluster participants share the conference with other clusters, meeting as a cluster only at the end of the event to establish their meeting schedules. Facilitators can opt for attending the whole event with their cluster members or joining them on the second day for their first cluster meeting (the facilitators have already been through the material).

4. Cluster calendar. The clusters are encouraged to meet six to eight times annually and provide an annual learning event that is coproduced by the cluster core for their larger leadership constellation.

5. Duration. The cluster will meet for two years with an annual covenant renewal. The renewal clause allows for clusters to disband if the experience is not producing a positive learning benefit. Frequently several months are required for clusters to gel, to form relationships that will bear the weight of freighting life learning at a deep level. After two years we intend for the cluster to reproduce into two or more new clusters. Each of the original cluster participants, individually or in teams, can serve as facilitator of a new cluster. The new clusters will have the same design and follow the same process as the original cluster. We do not force clusters to disband. Some relationships that develop in these groups will prove to be lifelong in duration. Many of those who choose to create new clusters still hold reunions of their original clusters.

6. Curriculum. Clusters basically create their own learning paths with some facilitation and guidance. Most of us have a shelf or two in our office containing the notebooks of stimulating conference experiences which we were certain we would revisit. Good intentions ran into ministry realities, and the notebooks collect dust. Our cluster process affords an intentional plan to pull the launch notebook off the shelf and review the contents. The notebook segments address four key areas confronting contemporary church leadership: paradigm issues, leadership micro-skill sets, resourcing strategies, and personal life development. The material synthesizes information in order to provide the learner with a litany of right questions in each of these areas. Because of this design the process of revisiting this material yields fresh learning and insights each time. In this way the curriculum serves primarily as a point for leaders to begin unpacking their experiences. The cluster facilitator covenants to lead the cluster to explore each of these areas at least once a year. This commitment is designed to keep the cluster from bogging down in any one area and to keep pushing the learning curve across the entire leadership landscape. The facilitator training notebook contains an illustrated two-year cluster learning path to help the facilitator think through the group's learning path (also included in the appendix). The curriculum contents reflect the bias of a missional paradigm for new apostolic churches and leaders.

C. Cluster Management and Administration

In our process we assume the following responsibilities at the state convention level.

1. Recruitment. We apply a basic leadership principle here. If you convince a group of leaders of the merits of an idea or proposal, you cannot keep it from happening. Leaders will see that the project comes about, no matter the obstacles. That is why we focus our energies in cluster development on recruiting the cluster facilitators. Once a leader captures the vision of this process, he or she will commit readily to the partnership.

2. Coaching. We also take responsibility for coaching the facilitators in their efforts. This coaching begins with a half-day training session designed to help them get started (most of this material is included in the appendix). After the clusters have been meeting for a few months, the facilitators reconvene for a coaching session to debrief their cluster experiences. By then they have real life issues and situations in their groups that are creating new learning needs for them as cluster leaders. This coaching session combines vision-casting and sharing among the facilitators about what is working for them and what is not. They mentor each other in their facilitator role. Testimonies serve to encourage them. Generally some leadership-skill-building or cutting edge insight is shared with them as a value-added feature (their "pay") of the coaching meeting.

3. Accountability. We have worked this into our system in a variety of ways. The facilitators communicate about their meetings mostly through a reporting process that flags their concerns or particular problems. We respond to those. We note which learning areas the clusters visit. We offer some financial help for producing the learning constellation events so we can monitor these events and provide coaching if necessary. Our system could be improved if more proactive contact could be sustained from our end. This aspect of the relationship between the facilitator and our convention team proves the most challenging. In the long run the consistency of learning quality may come to depend on the level of accountability that is maintained. In our third year of clustering, we added into the system a coach with more proactive responsibilities. Eventually we will devise some method for determining the impact of the cluster experience on the participants' leadership and congregation. We are committed to a process that produces results in terms of promoting the emergence of apostolic leaders and churches.

D. Cost and Funding

Our convention has a ministry partnership, a strategic alliance, with the Baptist Healthcare Systems of South Carolina. As a corporate donor and sponsor, Baptist Healthcare underwrites much of the cost of operating the cluster process. Their impact can be seen in the several ways. The JOSHUA PROJECT conference is subsidized for participants. Facilitators' training is provided to them at no charge. We provide the cluster launch conference to participants at no charge (including housing and meals). We offer a per registrant subsidy for the multi-congregational constellation conferences. This is done for two reasons. First, we do not want to place the learning leader in a position to be sabotaged at home by budgetary issues created by producing the constellation event. Second, the subsidy is provided after we receive information on the constellation conference (a report is included in the facilitator's notebook). This promotes accountability. We offer a "couples celebration" subsidy to encourage the cluster quartets to plan at least one event each year in which spouses are included. Our motive is to foster fellowship and support for ministers' spouses. We may not need to continue all these various funding supports once the value of cluster learning is firmly established.

E. Futuring

Several possibilities intrigue us for the future.

1. Distance learning. We intend to eventually deliver some convening instruction or curriculum through either satellite broadcast, video conferencing, or both. Instructional sites could be developed along the spine of a statewide counseling center network operated by Baptist Healthcare Systems. We would hope to have no church leadership more than one hour away from a learning center. Some consideration is being given to the development of a South Carolina intranet that would allow some kind of on-line learning possibilities. None of these applications would replace the need for skilled facilitators or take away the clusters' ability to determine their own learning paths. They would be developed as value-added features, especially useful for cluster launches or introducing new curriculum units. Eventually clusters will be able to order from a curriculum menu offered on CD-ROM. Again, such delivery systems mostly involve disseminating information. Real learning occurs when experiences can be unpacked with guided debriefings.

2. Tracking and measuring. We also want to create a tracking system that assesses both quantitative and qualitative measures in the congregations that are involved in cluster learning. The goal is to measure the impact of cluster learning on the participants' churches.

The appendix contains many of the support pieces that have been developed for use in our cluster learning process. These items, along with the explanation of our system in this chapter, are offered for two reasons: first, to prove that a learning community design that involves multi-congregational leadership can be developed and implemented, and second, to stimulate your thinking about the possibilities for your own involvement in such a process.

That is the next topic for our discussion.

5.

HOW DO YOU JOIN THE LEARNING REVOLUTION?

You need no more persuasion. You are ready to join the revolution. As a local church leader you know that new leadership challenges demand new leadership skills and insights. You feel overwhelmed by all you need to know. You like the idea of pushing your learning curve with other leaders who face the same dilemma. Besides, it is lonely where you are.

You are ready to get started. But how? Do you have to wait for your denomination or somebody else to develop a cluster learning model? What can you do? Plenty.

Getting Started with Your Learning Cluster

My own first experience with this learning approach was as a new pastor in a brand new church start in the mid-1980s. Four former schoolmates and I found ourselves in very similar situations. Each of us had completed our seminary education but realized quickly that our academic credentials fell far short of qualifying us as leaders of our congregations. We each had landed in Texas in similar ministry situations: three of us in new churches and two in congregations desperate enough for renewal to allow the implementation of new ministry approaches. Each situation called for strong pastoral leadership. Our lines of credit with our congregations were hefty but could be diminished rapidly with costly mistakes on our parts. We were in what was to us unchartered territory and did not know where to turn for help. Each of us understood that the culture was somehow shifting significantly. Though we did not know exactly how the church needed to respond, we were convinced that business-as-usual would certainly result in a diminished effectiveness in the church's mission. We had all kinds of ideas and were willing to try new approaches. We felt little denominational blessing for our innovative notions. This was before challenging the status quo was in vogue.

We decided to attend a three-day conference together. Those days were the height of the church growth movement, and the Charles E. Fuller Institute was conducting "Breaking the 200 Barrier" seminars all over the country. We convened in Dallas for three days, sat through the seminar together, lunched with Carl George (the director of the Institute and main presenter), and, at his suggestion, devised a game plan to continue our learning. The stimulation of the seminar and our time together was something none of us wanted to lose.

For the next several months we met in Dallas (because it was a central location) one Friday each month. Two of us drove two hours each way for the meeting. The fellowship was worth the drive to us. We took turns sharing what we were implementing in our churches from the Fuller seminar. In effect we were debriefing our shared learning experience with real-life ministry cases serving as the convening curriculum. During those months we worked on a wide range of issues, including worship service content and formats, preaching topics, personal schedules, local church conference planning, and philosophy of ministry statements. As we individually prepared to conduct leadership training events in our churches, we knew our colleagues would review our material and improve it when we met. This kind of mutual mentoring emboldened us to pursue more intentional ministries.

As we worked together, something else happened. We became friends. Some of us knew others in the group better than others when we initially got together. Some of us did not know each other at all. Our affinity was our similar ministry challenges and a commitment to learn, to go back to school in leadership. The hope that we would develop lifelong friends was not the driving motivation, yet that happened at different levels among some of our group.

Our spouses took note of the benefits we were drawing from our time with each other. Some began to express their own sense of isolation and loneliness and a desire to experience something like we were. Eventually they joined us twice a year for meetings as couples. Some of these times we had a planned learning agenda. On other occasions we met for fellowship and sharing. This continued until new ministry assignments scattered us across five states. For two years the five couples vacationed together. Some still do.

Even though our group met regularly as a learning group for only about two years, our leadership behavior was forever changed and our lives enriched. These were serendipitous results of the learning community we developed.

These experiences are recounted here for a couple of reasons. First, you need to know that what this book proposes really works. Second, you need to be released from waiting on someone else to make arrangements for you. Take the initiative. Decide now to create your own learning community. The rest of this chapter offers you some tips on getting started.

As you consider convening your learning cluster, the most critical factor for success will involve your determining the appropriate affinities to consider in recruiting. The most significant affinities to choose from include your ministry situation, your ministry philosophy, the size of your congregation, the age mix of churches and cluster members, and location. You do not have to match at each point. Our original group had several of these working for us. We all had similar ministry opportunities and ideas about how we wanted to go about ministry. We were all about the same age. In our case the sizes of our congregations varied and locations were spread out over a four hour drive. Your particular affinity mix may differ.

Approach prospective learning partners with a great deal of intentionality. Outline your desired outcome to them and how you plan to get there. Do not lower the bar in terms of the commitment you seek in order to attract a reluctant participant. You cannot afford to give a slot to someone who is not serious or who will not contribute to the process. Your learning team will only be as strong as the contributions of each member.

When recruiting you might mention mutual support as an expected benefit of the experience. However you probably do not want to emphasize this point. First, many ministers are threatened by venues that probe personal life issues. If they feel this is the primary focus of the group, many will decide not to become vulnerable through their participation. A climate of trust and affirmation has to develop to support life-changing environments. Developing this group ethos takes time and cannot be assured too soon. Second, if your cluster begins as a support group, it becomes more difficult to move to a more structured learning agenda. Cluster members coming primarily to receive support may not be willing to give the requisite energy to being a learning partner.

If you are following the proposed architectural plan for a learning cluster, you will need to decide about including multi-congregational conferences as part of the process. Our initial learning community experience did not include this feature. We have built this design piece into our statewide denominational plan for two reasons. First, our learning curve is steepened when we share what we learn with others. This is why teachers consistently say they get more out of their lessons than do their students. Second, we believe a congregation's leadership needs to be on the same page in order for significant organizational change to take place. One way to encourage behavior modification that results in significant change is to face issues together with others who confront similar challenges. Twelve-step groups have known and practiced this principle as a key part of their successful strategy to modify participants' thinking and actions.

You will want to consider a shared learning experience for your group very early on in your life together. This could even be an initial launch event (our practice). The event may be a conference sponsored by your denomination, a parachurch organization, a teaching church, or an individual consultant. You might also consider one- or two-day training events sponsored by colleges, universities, health organizations, or management groups. Another option is to view videos together or share audio cassettes in preparation for a meeting. The shared learning experience will put your group on a fast-track in terms of group dynamics and perhaps provide a curriculum around which to convene. Beginning with a shared set of learning material helps to mature the discussion dynamics and debriefing skills of the group. There is another advantage to beginning the cluster's learning by huddling over material developed by someone not a part of the group. The discussions will more likely be less tentative than if the initial focus zooms in on the ministry agenda and performance of cluster members. Let the group gel around learning stimulated from outside sources. Once rapport is established the interactive energy becomes available for group problem-solving and peer mentoring.

You will want to set aside a minimum of two hours for your cluster meetings. Some groups will prefer to include a fellowship time over breakfast or lunch. How will you use that time? Here are several suggestions. Vary the agenda depending on the day's learning objectives. The group may discuss a print piece or video resource. These can be reviewed together or each member can be responsible for debriefing the group on a different resource. Case studies also offer good learning opportunities. Members can take turns bringing issues to the table. Sometimes the approach of focusing on one participant each meeting guards against one or two dominant personalities using up all of the group energy each time. Praying for each other is always an appropriate way to spend some of the time together. Stay flexible. Be sensitive to the needs that may have emerged since the last meeting. Be sure to establish the learning goal and clear assignments for your next meeting.

Most groups will want to set monthly meetings as a goal. In reality this will work out to six to eight meetings a year given holidays and vacations. Less frequency in meetings will make it difficult for group dynamics to develop and for the energy to be maintained. We have at least one cluster that gets together each week. One of our groups meets on the Internet between face-to-face encounters.

Remember, everyone in the cluster needs to contribute to the learning. This means that members make the group a priority through their attendance and by accepting and completing learning assignments. One of the mistakes clusters make is in not establishing a high expectation in this regard. For instance, commitment to notifying the group facilitator of an absence ahead of the meeting is essential. These issues are best handled through a covenant agreement signed in each others' presence at the first meeting. Deal with any slippage when it occurs. This will preserve the relationships in the group from becoming unnecessarily bruised.

Breakfast for Champions (Lunch and Dinner, Too)

Curriculum for your learning community will mostly serve to convene your group. Once together your learning will serendipitously go beyond the convening piece. However, it is important to map out a learning path that visits key points of interest for effective church leaders.

Leadership for a new apostolic era pays attention to four basic areas of concern: paradigm issues, leadership micro-skill development, resourcing, and personal life development. Selecting from a menu of study in each of these areas provides a well-balanced leadership diet. The facilitators of the learning clusters in our system make sure their clusters visit each area at least annually.

The next four chapters provide you with a litany of issues in each of these areas that prove to be the most critical for apostolic leaders.

In other words, dealing with these issues will assure you that you are focusing on the twenty percent of questions that will make eighty percent of the difference in what you are trying to accomplish. Your cluster could review these menu offerings and make selections for in-depth learning. The outlines offered are designed to provide an exploration path for your cluster to examine the most critical elements in each area.

The following questions are the questions you need to be asking. By asking them in community, you will get better answers than you could come up with on your own.

6.

PARADIGM ISSUES

I f you are a minister who views your role as an enabler, you had better check your ministry paradigm. Church leaders of the future will be initiators. The ability to perform ministry rites, fill ministry roles, and preside over church activities will qualify you for the twentieth-century church. Twenty-first century church leaders will be evaluated on results. Character, competence, Christian commitment, and call rank ahead of academic credentials in the qualities required in today's leaders. Worship geared only for Christians or for seekers is giving way to worship evangelism. Evangelism is shifting its goals away from scoring a decision to securing a disciple. Leaders who view church members as obliged to support the church are in for a shock; effective twenty-first-century churches figure out ways for the church to serve its members. The list of paradigm shifts goes on and on.

Checking Your Paradigms

No effective leader at the turn of the millennium can ignore the issue of paradigms and the important role they play in the leadership challenge. Paradigms inform both vision and values in people and in organizations. They drive actions as well as influence attitudes. They serve as filters for how the world (processes, problems, and so forth) is perceived by the paradigm holder. In short, paradigms define reality for both leaders and followers. This dynamic is why it is so difficult for leaders and organizations to discern the future. This is also precisely why leaders have to pay attention to paradigm issues, especially checking out their existing paradigms to see if they match emerging realities.

Paradigms can and do shift. The changes that precipitate these shifts can be either gradual or abrupt. The pressure to shift paradigms can come from either outside or inside the person or organization. The shift may be perceived by people or organizations as positive or threatening. Whatever the impetus or circumstances, paradigm shifts always reflect the same bottom line: the rules of the game have changed. Previous actions or values, once unquestioned, now may be suspect, considered counter-productive, or no longer tolerated because they violate the new rules.

Paradigm shifts are accompanied by conflict. These conflicts may play out in one of several different scenarios. Sometimes the ambiguity leading up to the paradigm shift may produce a level of conflict that drops off once the breakthrough has been achieved. Or the opposite dynamic can occur. The introduction of a new paradigm may set off a maelstrom. This is often the case in organizational shifts if the leadership regime challenges deeply ensconced behavioral and attitudinal tenets of corporate culture.

Consider, for instance, the paradigm shift from a traditional church ministry to an apostolic church. A church leader ready to make this transition has often experienced a great deal of inward conflict, which has prepared him or her to shift ministry agendas. However, this point of emotional relief for the leader may just be the beginning of conflict for the congregation he or she leads. This is especially true when transitioning a traditional church into an apostolic church paradigm. The difficulty of this task can be seen in the number of pastors and staff leaders who decide to leave existing congregations to start new ones, and in the number of forced resignations and outright terminations of pastors and staff where this issue is the precipitating cause, whether or not it is cited as the presenting issue.

The subject of paradigms and paradigm shifts has captured the attention of business, education, and political leaders since Joel Barker and Stephen Covey popularized the concept in their books and videos. As the issues surrounding this topic have been discussed, several key principles have emerged that are repeatedly observed.

1. Paradigm pioneers usually arise from the edge, not from the center of the existing paradigm. Voices from the edge should be heard and evaluated, not ignored or dismissed. Paradigm shifters commonly hear phrases like, "We've tried it that way before, and it didn't work," or "We've never done it like that before," or even, "It's against policy."

2. The optimal time to search for a new paradigm is while the old one is still successful. This is easier said than done. Once plateau and decline have set in, the energy and resources needed to move to the new paradigm might be harder to marshal.

3. Paradigm paralysis occurs when an individual or organization holds on too tightly to one paradigm. Several factors contribute to this tendency: past success of the paradigm, our penchant to manipulate information to conform to what we are "supposed" to see, and an unwillingness or lack of readiness to change.

4. Projecting the past into the future proves fatal to those who want to survive. We are at a hinge point in history where the future will look very different from what has preceded it. Plans that perpetuate the known present into the future are deadly because they lull an organization into a false belief that it is prepared for the challenges and opportunities on the way.

5. When a new paradigm breaks through everyone goes back to zero. In other words any leverage held in the old paradigm is forfeited. This means the reactive leadership must be replaced with leadership that anticipates new realities.

The church, in many cases, has lagged behind in dealing with paradigm issues. Increasingly, as tectonic cultural shifts continue to make their impact, churches and church leaders can no longer avoid ministry paradigm issues. To not decide is a decision in today's world. That truth itself represents a paradigm shift brought about by the chaos of the times.

In commenting on these paradigm principles, Carol Childress of Leadership Network has suggested that church leaders should ask some key questions. These include:

• "What perceptions about the past keep us from seeing the present? What perceptions about the present keep us from seeing the future?"

• "Do our present paradigms allow us to fully minister to the diversity of our congregation and reach the unchurched population?"

• "How do our theological paradigms shape our methodological paradigms?"

• "Where is our church most vulnerable to be by-passed if the rules change and we go back to zero?"[1]

This book argues for some specific, major paradigm shifts that must occur if the church is to respond appropriately to new ministry opportunities in the new millennium These include:

• the shift to an apostolic leadership model for church leaders

• the shift from a refuge mentality to a mission mentality in church ministry approach

• the shift to a kingdom focus away from churchianity

• the adoption of the learning community as a methodology for ministry preparedness

Paradigm pioneer church leaders are positioning themselves to embrace these shifts. They realize that exegeting culture is an appropriate leadership function and responsibility.

Your Cluster at Work

Paradigm issues comprise one major issue that effective church leaders must address. A learning community of apostolic leaders will target this subject for discussion. If your learning cluster wanted to tackle this at one of your sessions, what could that time together look like?

For purposes of illustration let us adopt for the cluster's discussion the portion of chapter 2 in which we identified four paradigm or dimensional shifts in church ministry that would occur if the implications of universal priesthood were implemented (pages 39-42). Here is the outline that distills that discussion and could serve as a convening curriculum piece for the cluster.

Four Paradigm Shifts Acknowledging the Priesthood of All Believers

1. From top-down to flat line ministry
Issue: Who is empowered for what?
Typical answer: clergy-driven/dominated ministry
Missional approach: all believers empowered and equipped for ministry

2. From inside to inside-out
Issue: Where is the front for kingdom expansion?
Typical answer: church property and church programs
Missional approach: wherever Christian believer-priests have primary assignment, for example, homes, schools, workplaces, relational neighborhoods, and so forth

3. From outside to outside-in
Issue: Are we operating with the mission (customer) in mind?
Typical answer: "Come and get it!"
Missional approach: "We will meet you where you are!"

4. From the edge to the center
Issue: Where do we look for God to be at work?
Typical answer: God is at work in the church
Missional approach: God is also at work in the world, calling Christians to follow after him there.

One possible approach for your cluster's dealing with this material might involve each member of the cluster taking one of the above shifts as an individual learning assignment. Ahead of time they could work through the following litany of questions, recording their own ideas as discussion starters for the group time.

1. Do I agree with these characterizations of typical and missional approaches?

2. Which category more accurately reflects my current ministry practice?

3. What philosophical and theological challenges do these paradigm shifts pose for me?

4. What organizational concerns and impacts do I need to anticipate being affected by these shifts (budget, programs, calendar, worship, and so forth)?

5. What organizational behaviors need to change in light of these paradigm shifts?

6. What leadership role do I have for introducing these paradigm shifts to my congregation?

7. What personal behavioral changes would I need to make in order to shift paradigms in these areas?

8. How can I successfully manage the transition process in order to assure a successful implementation of these new approaches to ministry?

9. What resources have I found most helpful in working through this arena of thought?

10. How will I know that I am making progress? What would effectiveness in making these shifts look like?

11. What goals, projects, leadership activities, and behaviors am I willing to be held accountable for in order to begin applying my learnings?

Between now and _____ I will:

(1) _____

(2) _____

(3) _____

12. Gleanings from cluster discussion.

Working through this material may require several cluster meetings of two to three hours each. As an option the cluster could decide to do an overnight retreat. The learners choose their own speed because they are directing their learning. If a group of motivated learners worked intentionally through this material, some wonderful things would occur. Among them would be the following:

1. A significant evaluation of personal and organizational values and vision would occur. This addresses the most critical leadership task—self-understanding. Examining the unexamined can be revolutionary.

2. A synergy among the cluster participants would result in better thinking by the group than any individual in the group could bring to the issue alone. Insights by peers would sharpen both reflection and strategy.

3. The courage to change behavior would emerge, encouraged by the twin engine dynamics of group support and goal-setting.

4. More areas of needed learning would be identified. Perhaps the cluster would move to a study of the necessary leadership micro-skills for managing change and transition. Or the members might probe personal life issues, such as how they handle personal criticism.

5. Strategies would emerge for making the necessary paradigm shifts for greater missional effectiveness. This, in turn, would allow cluster members to coach each other into better leadership practices. One strategy might include making these four dimensions of paradigm shifts the focus for a multi-congregational leadership constellation conference.

6. Leadership insight and skill would be genuinely enhanced.

7. Congregational ministry approaches would become more intentional.

Could this learning path be travelled individually? Yes, but how many of us are willing to go it alone? And what happens to you or to your colleagues when challenges and dangers present themselves? Some go down with no one to launch a search and rescue mission. Some difficulties could be avoided altogether if another set of eyes looked at the situation. Some wilderness wanderings do not have to take a generation to complete.

Unfortunately, we have made the lone pathfinder the model for church leadership. The results, in terms of ministry losses and ineffective church responses to current ministry challenges, argue for a different preparedness model—learning communities.

This chapter has focused on paradigm shifts. Adopting a learning community approach to your own leadership development is itself a paradigm shift for most church leaders. Should you decide to make the transition, you will find others willing to go with you. Some of them cannot frame the issues or needs as well as you. However, once you invite them on the journey, they will soon recognize it is what they have been searching for.

7.

LEADERSHIP MICRO-SKILLS

W hat is in your leader toolkit? What are the key leadership micro-skills that leaders in a new apostolic era need? The standard issue toolkit for church leaders includes a Bible; a homiletics text; commentaries; seminary class notes; a denominational, church-year calendar; perhaps a seminar notebook or two on some aspect of church growth methodology produced by a parachurch organization, teaching church, or well-known speaker; and a subscription to a journal or two. By way of analogy, this level of preparedness would be akin to the shade tree mechanic unequipped with and untrained by computer technology. The well-meaning mechanic can do some basic maintenance and a certain level of diagnostics but that is about it. You would not characterize this level of competence as mechanical expertise adequate for working with today's sophisticated automobile systems.

Your Leader Toolkit

This chapter details some of the new specific pieces that will be needed in the toolkits of church leaders who want to be prepared for the next Christian millennium. Already we have identified new apostolic leaders as visionary, missional, empowering, team-oriented, entrepreneurial, and driven by kingdom values (see chapter 1). We have noted some of the special competencies that will distinguish effective twenty-first-century leaders from the rest of the pack. These included visioning capabilities, intuition, risk taking, systems thinking, opportunity making, trust, developing support (again, see chapter 1). The discussion of this chapter combines both of these previous explorations into a list of the most crucial tools the apostolic leader must have in terms of skill set mastery.

Self-understanding. The single most vital piece of information a leader needs is an understanding of who he or she is. Without this insight the leader eventually becomes ineffective. The other competencies that follow in this list will have validity only as they emerge out of a leader who has come to grips with himself or herself. In its essence the leadership journey is a personal one. An inner expedition must be accomplished foremost if life crusades involving others are to prove rewarding. Confident leadership relies on introspection into a number of arenas: family of origin issues, talent and gift assessment, personality strengths and weaknesses, personal mission definition—to name a few major areas for investigation. This fertile field can be cultivated through a variety of methods. A number of leadership instruments and inventories have been developed and provide immediate insight into many personal leadership dimensions Honest 360-degree feedback is considered valuable by any growing leader. The key pursuit here is for the leader to determine how to improve abilities to be the best leader possible in order to realize the congregation's best future.

Visioning. Leaders lead from the future. That is the domain of leaders. While some live in the past or try to recreate it, and while others accept the present as the way it will always be, leaders are drawing up plans and supervising bridge-building projects to link the present with a better future they have seen.

Unfortunately, when the need for visionary leadership is mentioned to church leaders, many call up images of Moses stepping down from Sinai with the tablets. Some church growth emphases over the past two decades have fed this unfortunate "voice of God" approach to vision. Because this type of experience falls outside the realm of experience for most church leaders, they often feel incompetent and defeated if this is their notion of what it means to provide visionary leadership. A lot of debugging needs to be done on this issue accompanied by an expanding attention to the processes of vision cultivation (personal and organizational) and vision casting (giving attention to both frequency of vision casting and forums). The visioning process must be demystified for many leaders. At the same time appropriate attention needs to be given to the spiritual nature of this skill.

Team Building. Very little in our culture instills in us the qualities of teamwork. Actually, the opposite is true. Our culture values individual accomplishment more highly and promotes individualism. We compete against others for grades, for dates, for jobs, for promotions, and for trophies of all kinds.

Any hope that circumstances are different in the Christian community is unfounded. In the church culture we have built an ethos of stardom, revolving around the pastor. Though it is entirely appropriate to acknowledge the leadership role of the pastor, we sometimes promote the notion that the church rises and falls on the pastor alone. This is a dangerous myth, the cause of ruinous attitudes and expectations both on the part of pastors and parishioners.

Effective leaders build teams around them. This can and should involve church staff relationships. However, many pastors with staff have not acquainted themselves with team building skills. The need for team building is not limited to leaders in multi-staff congregations. All pastors and staff need to practice team building with lay leaders. The inability to create a genuine sense of team between staff and key lay leaders often blunts the effectiveness of many churches.

Practical ministry considerations are not the only reason that team building qualifies as an essential leadership skill. Significant theological truths—including the mystery of the trinitarian nature of God, the body of Christ, and the doctrine of the universal priesthood of all believers—validate a team approach to ministry.

Mentoring and Coaching. A micro-skill related to team building is the ability of the church leader to mentor or disciple other leaders. The importance of this leadership in the church goes all the way back to Jesus and Paul. The Christian movement was born and nurtured by two men who placed obvious high value and methodological confidence on coaching others.

The difference between telling people what to do (an unavoidable function of leadership occasionally) or leading from the platform and becoming involved in face-to-face, heart-to-heart mentoring is significant. A performance oriented church culture has valued public leadership skills and rightly so. More recently, however, attention has been given to this more private, but powerful, dimension of leadership. Vulnerability and toughness, patience and prodding, prayer and persuasion all converge in the coach.

Communication. Communication skills in an information age can hardly be overrated in their importance for effective leadership. This skill set involves much more than podium prowess. The competency includes all forms of communication and media, written as well as spoken, verbal and nonverbal, public and private. The range of abilities extends from being able to decipher cultural trends to discovering congregational concerns through listening efforts. It involves sharing information in multiple venues and a variety of mediums. Developing an effective church communication infrastructure is as critical for missional performance as is the congregation's ability to communicate its message to its community.

Systems thinking. Very few church leaders are introduced to, much less taught, systems thinking. A failure to comprehend congregations through this filter can lead to unpleasant surprises. Actions taken in one area of church life have implications for others. These connections are not always apparent. For instance, creating new ministry ventures affects the facilities capacity, the fellowship system, and caring infrastructure simultaneously, perhaps creating a different impact than desired or even anticipated. Systems thinking, because it understands the interrelatedness of these systems, would much less likely be caught off guard. Another insight from systems thinking helps the informed leader know that desired outcomes are not always generated by what appear to be obvious linkages. Creating more parking may not be the only issue in a strategy to boost attendance, but the inventory of available parking cannot be neglected in considering a plan of action.

Managing corporate culture. Every church develops a corporate culture, replete with rituals and taboos. The effective leader must understand the culture of the organization in which she works. Elements of a church's cultural ethos include style, climate, communication patterns, decision-making processes, the formal and informal power structure, the demographics and psychographics of both the church constituency and the community, denominational affiliation, congregational traditions, myths, symbols, its orientation to the past and future, and more. Wise leadership accurately assesses corporate culture in planning and knows how to create a more innovative climate.

Leading change and transition. No organization or church can survive these turbulent times without successfully navigating the white water of change and transition. These two dynamics are related but distinct. Understanding the nature of transition and transition cycles may represent one of the least grasped bodies of knowledge possessed by church leaders. On the change side of the equation, the way change is introduced can spell the difference between success and disaster.

Conflict management and resolution. You need not ask *if* conflict will protrude into the church's agenda, but *when.* Of course the existence of conflict constitutes a sign of life. But too much can spell death, as attested by the pile of ministers' bodies mounting from forced terminations and the number of churches arrested in their growth. Most church leaders (especially pastors) are conflict allergic and tempted to pay too little attention to developing this micro-skill set. By not understanding the stages of conflict, church leaders often respond inappropriately, missing opportunities to defuse situations, on the one hand, or precipitating an escalation of hostilities, on the other.

Networking. Many church leaders fail to recognize networking as a necessary skill for the development of effective leadership practices. Isolated church leaders and congregations not only become stunted in their own growth, they inhibit the growth of the kingdom. The value of networking lies in the resources made available through exposure and relationship. Networking multiplies the number of potential solutions available to leaders, from problem solving to staff candidate resourcing. The lack of networking among church leaders reflects the independent and individual nature of current models of leadership development. The learning community approach offers a corrective to the lack of imagination and courage resulting from the atomization of church leaders.

Intuition. We would be hard pressed to find those among us who have ever taken an academic course on intuition. Yet intuition is widely regarded today as one of the most important attributes of twenty-first-century leadership. Against the widespread notion that intuition is something you either have or do not have, the truth is this cognitive process can be coached along. Spiritual leaders especially benefit from the development of intuition. Effective church leaders know there is more going on than meets the eye in congregational life. Two kingdoms are clashing. This is especially true for apostolic churches. The openness among leaders to developing intuitive skills is usually also accompanied by greater appreciation for and interest in the more mystical dimensions of the faith. Again, the learning community provides a safe place to test out intuitions and hunches before placing leadership credit on the line.

Interpersonal skills. Without exception the ability to get along with people ranks as the number one ingredient for success as a leader, no matter the venue. This does not mean that a church leader cannot be prophetic or challenge the status quo. The truth is, the leader's message has a better chance of finding home if he is well-positioned relationally. Not only do strong relationships prove helpful in creating an environment where personal spiritual challenges can be issued, they create a currency of trust during times when the leader must deliver difficult messages calling for congregational transformation. Love covers a multitude of sins. Congregations can forgive a lot if they love a lot. Leaders who genuinely exhibit caring and good people skills have a longer shelf life in congregations. The beginning place for the leader to develop interpersonal skills is a better self-understanding. That is why it is so important that church leaders pay attention to certain personal life concerns, including especially the insights grouped around family of origin issues.

Others would expand this list to add more critical leadership issues. Some would offer substitutions. The above discussion serves to highlight the skills most appropriate to the development of apostolic leaders. James Kouzes and Barry Posner, leadership consultants and authors, unintentionally describe the impact of apostolic leaders who would embody these abilities. Their audience is the American business culture, yet few among us in the church culture would not appreciate their elegant description:

> Beyond the horizon of time is a changed world, very different from today's world. Some people see beyond that horizon and into the future. They believe that dreams can become reality. They open our eyes and lift our spirits. They build trust and strengthen our relationships. They stand firm against the winds of resistance and give us the courage to continue the quest. We call these people *leaders*.[1]

Your Cluster at Work

Let us examine how a cluster learning session might approach one of these issues in leadership development. For purposes of illustration, we arbitrarily determine that the group has decided to spend a session studying vision. An outline of a learning agenda getting at this topic might look something like the following.

1. Background reading In preparation for the cluster meeting each member of the cluster would read one of the following: George Barna's *The Power of Vision*,[2] Bert Nanus's *Visionary Leadership*,[3]

or *The Visionary Leader* by Bob Wall, Robert Solum, and Mark Sobol.[4] Each might prepare a one-to-two-page summary of the book for the others or a summary of best quotes or most profound insights gained from the reading.

2. A list of discussion issues would involve:

(1) Cultivating vision. Each member would discuss frustrations, successes, and perspectives on vision cultivation practices.

(2) Casting vision. Each learner would be challenged to state a personal or church vision with attention to the use of various vision-casting forums.

(3) Cascading vision. Each participant would devise a plan to create vision ownership on the part of the leadership community.

Each learner would identify an area of ministry that needs revision and submit a plan to the group for coaching and accountability.

3. Goal setting for the group members would grow out of the discussion of the meeting and would vary according to the needs of the learners.

One could hardly be engaged in such an activity without coming away with new learning and new practices. This is how field-driven church leadership development will look in the third Christian millennium.

8.

RESOURCE MANAGEMENT

I magine an effective missional church that cannot raise money. Or, think of an apostolic congregation that operates without a vibrant prayer ministry. How about envisioning a highly dysfunctional staff team giving long-term leadership to a healthy congregation? Having trouble with these pictures? Of course you are. The marks of excellent leadership shows up not just in the leader, but throughout the organization for which the leader exercises stewardship.

An effective leader knows how to manage resources well. Even the most intelligent grasp of the future, coupled with clear understanding of the necessary paradigm shifts that must occur, does not generate an organization's performance by itself. Without proper resource management the only production that occurs is lively discussion. The ability to articulate a compelling vision for the church's future in and of itself may only raise expectations. It takes an intentional resource strategy to fuel the engine of change to take the congregation toward the desired destination.

Resource management skills represent a third area for learning in a balanced leadership diet. A couple of observations provide a backdrop for the discussion in this chapter. The first is that classic management skills come more into play at this juncture. A manager may not be a leader, but a leader may not escape being a manager.

Any effective leader is constantly in search of managerial insights that help to leverage her leadership efforts. A second observation points out the interrelated aspects of various leadership concerns. The manager role proves critical for fulfilling the leader's agenda in leading the church to greater ministry effectiveness. At the same time, the vision and values of the leader inform the management process. Apostolic congregations will have different managerial concerns than will refuge congregations.

In this chapter we take a look at a litany of learning questions that leaders of apostolic churches need to explore in key resource areas. Then we think through how a learning cluster session might tackle one of these issues

Your Essential Resources

The effective apostolic church leader will devise strategies to maximize the following key resources:

Prayer. The New Testament witnesses to the connection between prayer and apostolic leadership. The church was born during a multiple-day prayer meeting. Public miracle-working prayer was part of the apostolic expansion strategy. Home prayer meetings provided the strength to endure mounting persecution. Decisions were made in an atmosphere of prayer (Acts 15 conference). The church received direction for new ministry ventures through prayer (the commissioning of Saul and Barnabas in Acts 13). Some of Paul's writings yield insight into the prayer concerns of early apostolic leaders (Ephesians 1, 3). Even the most casual observer of the phenomenon of the early church expansion cannot miss the vital link between prayer and the power for kingdom growth.

The emerging generation of leaders for a new apostolic era will also evidence the same spiritual dynamic. They will unashamedly admit their dependence on the Spirit. Their lives will be unexplainable apart from prayer. Their utilization of personal prayer intercessors will reveal the strategic priority prayer occupies in their ministry. They will also marshal congregational prayer efforts in interceding for the work of God.

Apostolic leaders carry an enhanced sense of spiritual engagement that pits them and their churches against an enemy who resists their efforts. They understand that enlarging heaven means rescuing people from another existing kingdom. Prayer releases the power of God to weaken enemy positions. The old paradigm maintained that prayer was preparation for the battle. An apostolic prayer paradigm views prayer as the battle.

Staff and Leadership Team. Entire books devote themselves to this subject. Our objective here involves detailing a few key points that distinctly apply to apostolic leaders.

1. We have already asserted that the single most important piece of information a leader needs is self-understanding. This insight can hardly be overrated when it comes to building a leadership team. An unexamined life can wreak havoc on those obliged to live in its shadow. Self-understanding for apostolic leaders would involve a defining vision for his or her ministry. This vision will be as clear and captivating as Jesus' call was to his first-century followers. The apostolic leader possesses an honest appraisal of his or her own personality, talents, and spiritual giftedness. Only when this set of insights is in place can intentional team building replace haphazard recruitment strategies that do not result in complementing existing leadership.

2. Staff and leadership team members must shift from seeing their role as performers to seeing themselves as developers. Outmoded paradigms of staff ministry leaders view them as people employed to personally provide ministry programs. The minister of music and worship in this model has responsibility to lead choirs, sing solos, and personally lead the congregation in worship. After all, "That's what we pay her to do." Churches can no longer afford this kind of thinking. Apostolic ministry leaders recruit and deploy lay ministry teams, a model that exponentially expands the ministry effectiveness. In this approach the worship leader's task and job performance will be evaluated on her ability to discover, to equip, and to coach worship teams who will lead various worship services.

In addition, the worship leader will be entrepreneurially creating venues for worship and worship teams.

3. Most churches have more staff leadership available to them than they realize. In fact the "single-staff church" concept reflects both poor theology and bad leadership practice. Increasingly apostolic leaders will create teams of lay ministers in their congregations. They will recognize and validate the call of God on members' lives to give leadership to various church ministries. These lay ministry leaders will have the full level of accountability and authority generally associated with "professional" staff. Congregations that utilize bivocational, part-time, and token-pay leaders will find ways to "pay" these "employees" with far more than money: a chance to exercise their ministry passion and the ability to participate in ministry training and preparedness.

Lay ministry partners. Old paradigm thinking in this category views people as resources for clergy to use in building the church. The question expressing that mind-set is, What can people do to help the church succeed? In answering that question we have constructed an entire church culture around clergy-driven and clergy-led campaigns to access church members' time, money, and talent for church program efforts so that the clergy succeed.

An apostolic paradigm takes a different approach. People are seen as ministers which God develops for building the kingdom. The question emerging from this perspective reads, What can the church do to help people succeed in a missional lifestyle? The focus here is on people, not programs. The ministry agenda moves beyond church issues to kingdom concerns. Ministry venues move outside the church walls into the community.

Kingdom business is the people development business. Helping people discover their callings, passions, gifts, talents, and personal wiring frees them up to serve as God's priests on mission with him in the world. This is the primary goal of discipleship in apostolic congregations. This constitutes a very different discipleship objective from that of the typical church approach, which is mostly interested in raising up another group of workers to satisfy church program needs.

The church leader who understands his role in deploying God's people will establish a congregational ethos that promotes intentional people development. The development continuum would include assessment of gifts, passions, talents, and temperament. It would provide apprenticing opportunities to develop micro-skills in ministry leadership Adequate feedback for leadership growth would be given to those in leadership positions. A development or discipleship system would also provide adequate coaching and mentoring in life goal pursuits.

Time. Apostolic leaders use their time differently than typical ministers in two significant respects. The first can be seen by way of contrast. Old paradigm ministry approaches value time spent "doing" ministry. Effective church leaders in a third Christian millennium will spend more time "developing" ministry. This emphasis does not disparage hands-on ministry efforts. In fact it values the personal touch in a way that surpasses the usual practice. The apostolic leader is determined to increase exponentially the congregation's care capability through mobilizing teams of ministers within the church membership. The level of care increases in missional congregations. This approach makes sure that more ministry occurs than what only a few "professionals" can do. The second distinct way the apostolic leader uses time is in proactive planning for the church's future. This includes time spent in vision cultivation and vision casting with key leaders and constituencies to create a competent leadership core.

Jesus serves as a time priority model for apostolic leaders. With the whole world to touch, Jesus took time to develop the Twelve. He could have touched more had he not retreated with the apostles. Some probably even criticized him for rationing his power. Surely he himself faced enormous internal pressure and temptation to keep touching, to keep teaching, to keep healing, to deal with the urgent needs all around. Had he not managed his energy, he would have neglected the strategic time for developing the leaders who would carry his movement forward.

Money. No leader can ignore money issues without seriously jeopardizing his or her mission. What are some key areas of concern that the leader must pay attention to?

1. Pay attention to motivational bases for why people give and what they give to. The day of raising money by appeal to the church's organizational needs has very little light left in it. Key leaders, the ones who usually wind up on stewardship committees, frequently give from a different motivational base than does the average church member. Kennon Callahan observes that leaders generally give out of a sense of commitment and challenge whereas the average church member gives out of a sense of compassion and community.[1] The impact of these differing motivational bases for giving shows up in stewardship campaigns that fail to tap into the key motivational bases of most members of the congregation. Discerning why people give does little to affect the weekly offering unless money appeals are translated into their motivational language.

2. Pay attention to giving patterns. Giving patterns shift over time and from one location to another. The value of this information for leaders is that it helps give insight for decision making that impacts cash flow, morale, and timing. Stewardship campaigns should not be launched in the weakest giving months, for instance. Nor should budget receipts or expenditures be expected to distribute evenly throughout the year.

3. Pay attention to communication about money. People are particularly sensitive about communication regarding *their* money. What stewardship messages are sent from the pulpit and church publications? What is the tone of your language? Is expectation overbalanced by gratitude? Do people know how their stewardship is making a difference in people's lives? Are church members demoralized or affirmed? When are you in touch with the congregation about money? How are offerings and expenditures reported? What is the level of accountability for financial affairs of the congregation?

4. Pay attention to expanding revenue possibilities. Many congregations limit their income by failure to tap available revenue streams. Some operate with the outmoded concept "There is only so much money out there." In fact most congregations would benefit from more options, not fewer, in terms of choices available to donors.[2] Increasingly churches are considering availability and use of community funding streams, such as government and foundation grants, especially to finance the work of the congregation in community projects aimed at children, the elderly, and the poor.

The key lesson for apostolic leaders who want to expand financial resources is that people give to mission-driven causes where and when they can see the result of their giving in people's lives.

Facilities. Facility needs vary from place to place and from situation to situation. Apostolic leaders must be aware that in the past, building design and use were often dictated by church-based programming. In the new paradigm, building design and use will reflect a mission-driven agenda. Affordability, visibility, accessibility, flexibility, and expandability are all variables to consider in selecting the meeting space or spaces for your congregation. Cost effectiveness and church ministry configurations also play key determining roles. Too often church leaders rush to secure undesirable space that proves too limiting and begins to dictate ministry options. This trap can be avoided if careful deliberations consider the above-mentioned factors and remain purpose-driven.

Technology. Too often churches are late in adopting technology that could greatly improve their ministry effectiveness. Searching and sorting, calculating, word processing, graphics, planning, communications, research, worship enhancement, people tracking—this is just a starter list of areas that technology can contribute to the church's ministry. Computer technology is joined by the digital revolution to make possible communications that were viewed as science fiction only a few years ago. The ability to share information with congregational members and anybody else through the Internet, or intranet, venues is a whole new opportunity for entrepreneurial apostolic leaders. The distance learning capabilities will open up new options for what is considered the church "field." The old paradigm was to see technology as a tool to be used in supporting the church ministry. The new paradigm sees technology as a gift from God that creates entirely new ministry possibilities.

Prayer, staff and leadership teams, lay ministry partners, time, money, facilities, technology—these are key resources that leaders must manage effectively in leading apostolic churches. Leaders who fail to see these management challenges as opportunities will fail to maximize their potential. Each is critical. None can be neglected without negatively impacting ministry effectiveness.

Your Cluster at Work

A learning cluster may decide to devote one of its sessions to explore how the participants can maximize the resource of prayer. Each member could fill out the following items before the meeting and make additional notes during the discussion.

Need(s). Spell out the need or needs you have in this resource management opportunity. Do you need to develop a personal prayer support team? Be specific. Perhaps several needs will emerge. Each can be dealt with in this strategic and tactical analysis.

Barrier(s). Next to the need identify the major barrier or barriers that you perceive must be overcome in order to address the need. Is an imbalanced prayer focus keeping you from marshaling congregational efforts for kingdom concerns? Is there a personal barrier in your own prayer practice?

Cause(s). What contributes to the problem as best you can tell? Is there a lack of teaching on prayer or a lack of modeling? Does your communication infrastructure make it difficult to impact the congregation's prayer life? Is personal pride preventing you from asking for prayer support for your own ministry efforts?

Solution(s). Beside each cause scratch out possible solutions to consider. Would a class on the practice of intercessory prayer be helpful? Is this the time for a sermon series on the power of prayer in the kingdom of God? Does an organized prayer ministry need to be started or at least considered?

Action Steps. Each solution will call for action steps to get you from where you are to where you want to go. Perhaps church leaders need to be briefed, sermons preached, or prayer warriors recruited. This is tactical planning.

Time Lines. Every action step needs to have the built-in accountability of scheduling the activity. Drawing up a time line helps keep the leader on track for implementation as well as making it easier to delegate responsibility for implementation.

By the time the cluster concludes this analysis and planning, each participant will have his or her own ideas greatly enhanced by the other learners. The synergy of the discussion will also enhance the problem-solving capability of each member, a value-added feature of the intentional learning community.

9.

THE LEADER AS A PERSON

His rise was meteoric. Personal charm matched pulpit prowess. Everything Charles touched seemed to turn to gold. As his ministry grew, so did the hole in his soul. He became less and less accountable, and more and more insulated from the growing number of people who were always around. His isolation soon became complete, even from his family. In search of some intimacy to assuage his loneliness, he committed pastoral suicide. The affair ended his ministry.

Fred attends to his flock dutifully. In fact his whole ministry life has become a matter of duty. The joy has been gone for years. If he knew anything else to do, he would. At least he would have ten years ago. Now it is just a matter of hanging on until retirement. To wind up with this sense of insignificance and lack of spiritual power was not what he had expected when he answered the call to ministry.

About every three years the scene repeats itself. It is happening again, and Alan is almost as bewildered as his congregation. Things start out well enough, but the honeymoon only lasts a few months. Then one by one Alan finds himself on opposite sides of issues with different parishioners. The disagreements always seem to turn personal and the relationship becomes strained. The people never seem to understand Alan or appreciate his high commitment to work and to excellence. They always let him down and eventually he wears out his welcome. But Alan does not understand. He does not expect any more from the church members than he expects of himself.

Swap the names, change a few of the details, and we all know Charles, Fred, and Alan—ministers with great starts but poor endings; church leaders who died before they quit, living out their days as emotional zombies. These ministers play out a script they have not yet learned to read. These conditions only begin the list of professional hazards for those who answer the call to serve God by serving his people. Somehow, in helping others get a life, many ministers lose their own.

Ultimately the chief asset a church leader brings to the table is his or her own person. All of the brilliance or insight in the world cannot make up for a cratered personal life. Failure to pay attention to personal life development plots a course for disaster. Yet it seems that many church leaders ignore the personal dimensions of leadership development.

The results of this inattention are readily apparent. Research validates what anybody knows who works day in and day out with church leaders. As a group they are increasingly subject to burnout and depression. They struggle with diminishing self-esteem and family pressures. They are vulnerable to sexual temptation. They are lonely, find it difficult to share their pain, and, for the most part, decline to make themselves available or accountable for help. This growing clergy crisis proves one of the great barriers to genuine church renewal.

Critical Issues

This chapter raises a litany of questions church leaders should be asking themselves in the area of personal life and health maintenance. As in the three previous chapters, a concluding potential exercise for the learning cluster demonstrates the way this subject could be dealt with in that setting. In fact, no other area of investigation is more powerfully affected by the learning community approach than these personal concerns. Because the learning cluster targets changed behavior for positive growth, it naturally lends itself to an examination of personal life issues. The following areas constitute the most critical for leaders to consider in paying attention to their personal lives.

Spiritual Formation

Spiritual formation is the most significant issue facing church leaders for the future. This is true both for the congregational context as well as for the personal practice of the leader. Spiritual formation is the process whereby Christ is formed in us. This process includes the discipline and intentional efforts, which we practice publicly and privately, intended to open our lives to God for him to fashion his heart in us.

We evangelicals know precious little about this subject. Our workaholic and materialistic brand of Christianity so emphasizes production and power that we have a hard time getting in touch with the less glamorous and quieter work of the Spirit. We misguidedly check our attendance statistics, bank accounts, and impact on the polls for signs of our strength instead of discerning the level of life transformation occurring in our midst. In short, we know how to count but not how to measure. Is Christ being formed in us? Are we behaving like the body of Christ, or as a group observing civil religious rites and serving as moral watchdogs? Do we honestly love people or just want them to behave?

The challenge of spiritual formation extends beyond the approaches that typical congregations take. It includes the issue of how the faith is passed down from one generation to the next within the community of believers. In recent decades a spiritual formation agenda largely vanished to be replaced with programmatic activities and educational approaches to developing people. "Discipleship" became a program of education. The assumption was made that the secular educational model would serve as an adequate model for developing believers' spiritual lives. We further assumed that if people were immersed in church activities and programs they would emerge with Christian character somehow inculcated into them through osmosis. In this paradigm the busier a person was with church activity the more spiritual he or she was considered to be.

We now know that these assumptions were and are misguided. Spiritual formation cannot occur in someone's life without accountability. A classroom model aimed at transmitting cognitive information to hearers in small classes and large lecture halls (sanctuaries) does not typically dial accountability into the mix. (More contemporary words for the ancient idea of accountability include mentoring and coaching). We are born into families (and not into the class of 2000) partly to incorporate accountability into our lives. However, we are being left largely on our own in terms of spiritual development. As a result we are producing churches with members whose attitudes and practices vary little from the culture at large. The pseudo-community created by the media is a more powerful force in shaping values than years of sermons and lessons. Many churches are turning to small group ministries in an attempt to create community that makes a difference in people's lives.

Busier Christians are not necessarily more spiritual. They are just more tired and increasingly burned out on church programming. Many churches fail to come out of denial at this point because they have no other way of measuring than counting participation at church activities. Worse, yet, when people drop out of the frenetic pace of church life, they are considered somehow less committed to Christ. So we are creating untold numbers of guilty Christians who feel "less spiritual" than they "should be." As a result we are attempting to evangelize our culture with a demoralized work force. In worst case scenarios, Christians with a life agenda that can no longer be dictated by the church schedule are exiled out of being able to impact the church's ministry efforts. The only ones left are having a range of other social and psychological needs met by congregating at the church. This may in part explain the lack of external focus of many congregations

A further question of congregational efforts in spiritual formation needs to be considered by apostolic leaders. The approaches to spiritual formation are done differently when we think we are in charge than when we see ourselves as exiles in a foreign land. If we believe the church is part of the establishment, a predominant cultural force, we will count on other aspects of culture to prop up and reinforce our teachings. This is the Constantinian world order that has shaped our current spiritual formation tactics. If we embrace the reality that the community of believers is a band of pilgrims in a culture hostile to the faith, then spiritual formation efforts will become far more intentional.

Congregational ineptness at spiritual formation is mirrored in the individual lives of the congregants, including the leaders. The process of Christ being formed in us has largely been relegated to a private set of personal disciplines. The assumption, again, is that enough hours logged in at quiet time will pay off in changed behavior. The missing element in terms of affecting changed behavior has been the creation of appropriate venues for debriefing and accountability. The emergence of the cry for mentors and spiritual directors reflects a growing dissatisfaction with the return on investment of solo attempts at spiritual maturation. The learning cluster is tailor-made for addressing the spiritual formation process.

Balanced Personal Growth

Effective leaders cannot afford to ignore the full range of personal development. This includes not only the spiritual arena but also the areas of physical, intellectual, and emotional wellness. This is not easy to do given the work habits of ministers. The Alban Institute reports that ministers working over fifty hours per week over a sustained period typically suffer in at least one of three ways (1) They lose their spiritual vitality. (2) They experience a relationship deficit because they have no time to nurture these. (3) They neglect their bodies with negative physical consequences.[1] A learning cluster provides the chance for some accountability in this area.

Cluster members could challenge each other to greater attention in these areas and coach each other in life health goals.

Physical maintenance poses a challenge for three primary reasons. First, as already mentioned, it takes time to look after one's body, and it is easy to neglect this in order to tend to other more immediately urgent matters. Second, a psychological battle rages in many ministers over what is seen as "selfish" behavior, taking time for personal physical maintenance. A guilt trip can occur in many clergy with very little provocation. Third, the lifestyle of those in ministry involves a lot of sitting, riding, and eating at church functions.

Intellectual growth can prevent stale-out, a condition that shows up in private conversations and in public speaking venues most noticeably. Church leaders who take their mind off-line begin showing signs within two years. The truth is, church members in many places tolerate the lack of intellectual growth because of relationship credits held by the minister. On the other hand, an intellectually-stimulated ministry team brings creativity and freshness to the church ethos.

The most challenging personal issue for ministers to deal with involves their emotional life. Ministers are treated to the entire emotional gamut, often compressed into a very short time period. It is a short walk in the hospital from the delivery room to the bedside of someone dying with cancer. Many church ministers have celebrated a new arrival and presided over a departure within minutes of each other. The emotions cannot be processed that quickly. And, often the pastor must postpone dealing with his or her grief while attending to the stricken family. The trouble is, the minister's time never comes, for there is always another crisis or occasion that calls for celebration or sympathy. Simply ignoring emotions does not dismiss them. They will be dealt with one way or another—healthily or unhealthily. Many church leaders (pastors, especially) are not skilled in maintaining their emotional health. Granted, some are at greater risk because of their own wiring. But across the board very little proactive help has been given to clergy to help them cope with emotional stress.

Too often ministers adopt one of two inappropriate ways of dealing with emotional toll. The first approach simply allows emotions to be drained out of the minister after taking hit after hit emotionally, with no allowance for emotional refueling. The result is emotional exhaustion. The most telling symptom is lack of joy. The second unhealthy approach to handling emotional turmoil involves the minister intentionally defending his or her emotional life. This is done through insulating oneself emotionally. This approach usually grows out of deep wounds that the leader has experienced. Because of their pain, they determine never to be vulnerable again. "I will never be hurt like that again," they say to themselves. The result is an arrested emotional development that shows up in emotional detachment. The number of emotionally aloof church leaders is legion.

The learning community, if it can become a safe place, can provide an opportunity for emotional health to be regained and maintained.

Family of Origin Issues

Part of the maturation process for any church leader involves an exploration of the legacy of his or her family of origin. Without this investigation the leader's self-understanding lacks an important body of insight. The leader's self-understanding, remember, is the single most critical piece of information a leader needs for long-term ministry effectiveness.

The significance of family of origin issues can easily be illustrated. Some leaders have unresolved conflicts with parents or family members, causing them to act out inappropriately. Oftentimes these leaders will not even be aware of how this underlying tension is hurting their work style or relationships. For instance, an overachieving church leader may be in fact still seeking a parental blessing. The search may push the leader into damaging work habits that threaten to destroy relationships with family or colleagues.

Family members, staff colleagues, and church members may feel from the leader high expectations they cannot possibly meet. The overachieving church leader pushes staff and congregation to exhaustion.

A family of origin examination may reveal insights into hidden addictions or compulsions in the leader. The "sins of the fathers" are passed down the generational chain. About 35 million people in North America have grown up in alcoholic families. Adult children of alcoholics (ACAs) are at high risk for emotional and behavioral problems. The rules they learn very early (do not talk, do not feel, do not trust, do not betray the family, keep the secrets) often get translated into adult life as: "Feelings are bad," "Do not trust others," "I must be perfect," or "I do not deserve anything good." ACAs respond to their childhood with behaviors that attempt to control themselves and their world around them. They adopt compulsive behaviors.[2] The addictions or compulsions of the ACA may have changed form from the previous generation. The driving forces may include food, sex, power, adrenaline, work, the need to be needed, or other drugs of choice.

Sometimes the leader may be unaware of the influence of these family of origin issues on his behavior. Often, recurring problems or crises in a church leader's ministry can be traced to an underlying psychological issue that prompts inappropriate behavior on the leader's part.

The reason for intensely searching family of origin issues is not so the leader can find out who to blame for his or her behavior. This would be a forfeiture of responsibility for his own choices. The goal is just the opposite: to allow the leader to assume more personal responsibility for her attitudes and actions. Otherwise, circumstances continue to push buttons and pull levers in the leader that prove hard to manage because they are not understood and named.

Personal Dragons

Certain troubling emotions or bundles of negative energy stalk many church leaders. These can be designated as personal dragons.

Not every leader will deal with all of these. Perhaps you do not wrestle with any, or your particular dragons may not be found in the listing in this section. However, the most fiercely challenging dragons for most church leaders are the following.

Depression. Many church leaders are depressed. Some of them do not even know it because its manifestation can take several forms. For those who consciously struggle with this beast, there is often a reluctance to seek help. They see depression as some sort of sin or failure. After all, are not successful Christians happy? Certain levels of depression signal a normal emotional response to the amount of emotional stimuli experienced by most church leaders. Treatment of the symptoms of depression can avoid its becoming an illness in itself. Many leaders feel they have to slay this dragon all on their own. Others believe that if they close their eyes and wish it away, depression will flee. Some leaders deny depression by giving it other names. The usual choice is "burnout".

Anger. This dragon is the most frequent companion to the first dragon. In fact they are related to each other. Ministers are vulnerable targets in an increasingly angry culture. They represent authority figures and God, frequent objects of anger for many dysfunctional people. Church leaders often carry some internal anger themselves, sometimes harboring and feeding what becomes their pet dragon for years. The list of who and what ministers are angry with covers a wide spectrum: God, the devil, their parents, their children, their spouse, their congregation, their denomination, the bishop, the elders, themselves. This dragon wreaks havoc on the soul.

Loneliness. Leadership at its heart is a lonely journey. However it can be made much lonelier than it needs to be. Many church leaders, for a variety of reasons, live in personally-imposed exile in the middle of their community of faith. This makes them vulnerable, especially to pornography (often representing a pseudo-intimacy) and extra-marital affairs.

Unrealistic Expectations. These can come both from the congregation and from inside the leader. A leader always struggles against unmet expectations. The challenge for the leader is to decide what is reasonable to allow others to expect or to expect of herself. The best strategies against this dragon involve honest confrontation with any codependent tendencies in the leader or congregation and establishing healthy boundaries.

Criticism. The fact that criticism goes with the territory apparently seems to escape many church leaders. This observation is based on the obvious lack of intentional strategy by many church leaders to deal with it in healthy ways. They allow the hot breath of this dragon to wilt them over time, apparently unaware that they can temper the heat with appropriate measures and protective gear. Some church leaders, especially small church pastors, have trouble with self-differentiation from their church ministries and therefore take every criticism to heart. The worst-case scenario occurs when criticism is mismanaged and a church-wide conflict is precipitated.

Guilt. This particular dragon lurks at the door of many church leaders, rarely giving those it affects any rest. Those stung by its barbs struggle with their own humanness or with a failure to receive God's forgiveness. Those susceptible often carry shame-based backgrounds. The guilt dragon shows up in a variety of ways in the leader, from legalism to narcissism to feelings of extreme low self-esteem.

Loss and Grief. Church leaders certainly face this dragon in the lives of their church members as they minister to them. Sometimes the monster follows them home. Many church leaders struggle with the loss of friends, money, prestige, security, family and personal time, personal dreams, and idealism—to mention only a few. Loss of some kind is unavoidable in life. However, the failure to grieve appropriately, or an arrested grief, invites the dragon to keep the leader's emotional house torn up.

Fear. A number of church leaders live with fear as a constant companion—fear of loss, fear of failure, fear of success. Fear is paralyzing. It constrains creativity and stunts ministry effectiveness. Leading from a fear vantage point diminishes the leader's vision. Over time, fear debilitates and shrinks the leader down to its size.

Family Relationships

This delicate area of personal growth presents many challenges to the church leader. In many arenas of society, the leader's family relationships do not necessarily come into play in terms of the leader's effectiveness. This is not so in the church. The family serves as a crucible of Christ-forming dynamics for the minister. Healthy family relationships give the Christian leader a decided advantage. Not only does the leader gain the emotional and spiritual strength that derives from them, the leader's credibility factor also increases dramatically when this area of life is obviously well managed.

Good family life does not just happen. It takes a lot of intentionality and proactive effort on the part of the church leader. Unfortunately too often the minister allows urgent needs to skew the priorities that are truly important.

Church leaders could make better allocations of energy and time if they had the support of a group. The cluster could hold them accountable for their growth in family relationships. Other cluster members could often share insights that would enrich the leader's home life.

The learning cluster is not designed as a therapy group, or even primarily as a support group. Groups for these purposes have existed for years, providing varying degrees of help to those who have participated in them. Yet many church leaders are reluctant to join these groups for a variety of reasons, most of which have to do with issues of pride, trust, and vulnerability. However, if personal health issues are addressed in the context of learning, the chances are improved that the church leader will grapple with them. Support will grow out of learning.

Your Cluster at Work

A cluster might choose to examine the balanced life of a leader, focusing on spiritual, physical, intellectual, and emotional growth. Whereas each of these areas introduces a wide range of issues, the following learning exercise could get the ball rolling to facilitate significant learning.

In preparation for the cluster meeting the participants could complete the following assignment individually:

(1) How would you rate your personal regimen in maintenancing yourself . . .

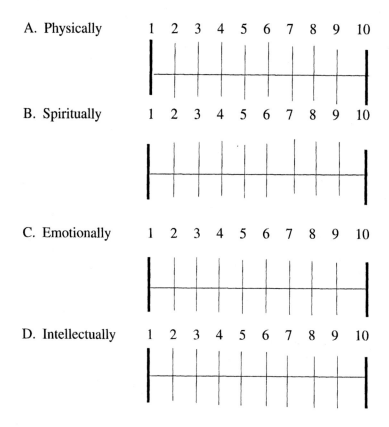

A. Physically   1   2   3   4   5   6   7   8   9   10

B. Spiritually   1   2   3   4   5   6   7   8   9   10

C. Emotionally   1   2   3   4   5   6   7   8   9   10

D. Intellectually   1   2   3   4   5   6   7   8   9   10

(2) Choose the lowest ranked category and develop a *realistic* action plan for growth over the next month.

Members would come to the cluster meeting prepared to share their answers. They would gain and give insight in developing part of a personal growth plan. They could then be coached through peer accountability into changed behavior. That is the power of learning in community.

10.

Denominational Players

God has given each denominational system the freedom to become completely irrelevant or to be a relevant servant of the churches. Each will choose. Future vitality will require that many (if not most) denominational organizations shift paradigms to deliver real, timely help to congregations and congregational leaders.

Strategies for Cluster Implementation

The learning cluster approach provides a way whereby denominations can be viable players in the future of leadership development. This chapter positions several road markers to show how denominations can facilitate the emergence of learning communities.

1. Create a climate for this new learning paradigm

A first step in developing the possibility for community learning involves creating the climate for the introduction of a new model. Depending on your position on denominational staff, you might first need to secure a corporate sponsor, someone with enough authority in your organization to empower your idea.

Assuming you have adequate sponsorship, the next move involves shopping the idea around. If your initial target group is pastors, one good kickoff plan would involve convening a group of visible pastors as an architectural and legitimizing group. They may adopt the plan wholesale as outlined in this book or modify some of its components. You can afford to be flexible in some details as long as key elements are retained. These key ideas include a minimum cluster size of three, the formation of the cluster along affinity lines, the covenant dynamic among members, and the commitment for the cluster to move beyond a member support function to an intentional learning path.

Once a legitimizing group has accepted the proposal, consider some visible forum where you can unveil the plan. From that point you will need to seize every opportunity for vision casting: denominational publications, leadership development events, and any meeting or gathering of pastors or staff leaders you can find or convene yourself. You might devise a plan for shopping the idea, including an intentional vision-casting campaign, by all members of the pastors' architectural group that helped you to draft the process.

You are not recruiting at this point. You are vision casting by rehearsing the leadership needs giving rise to this new learning paradigm and the benefits of the experience that you envision for those who will participate in the process. Be careful not to present this process as a new program. Local church leaders are wary of signing up for another denominational program. This concept must be perceived as a process facilitated by the denomination. Your role is to call the party. Only those interested in participating in a leadership development revolution need to show up. If your own line of credit is good with the church leaders, you will find a warm reception and eager questions. You may share a time line and alert them to consider their own willingness to participate in a cluster.

Begin to take notice of church leaders who seem particularly eager for the process to materialize. You will be compiling a list of potential facilitators from these encounters as well as a pool of cluster member candidates.

2. *Focus on creating a leadership pool*

The first impulse you may have is to begin recruiting cluster group participants. Resist that temptation. Instead, focus on creating a leadership pool of potential facilitators. Remember, if you develop leaders, you cannot keep something from happening.

Without question, the single most important ingredient to your process success is a right selection of facilitators. Consider high octane, highly motivated paradigm pioneer types as facilitators. Also think of relationally skilled pastors who can help create community. Depending on your context, you might consider theological diversity, geographic coverage, and a variety of ministry philosophies in order to assure a range of coverage when the clusters form. Or, you may choose to target a certain type of congregation for inclusion in the start-up process. The point is that you want to begin recruiting facilitators with the end in mind. The makeup of the facilitator leadership will determine the makeup of the clusters.

Consider creating a shared learning experience for the potential facilitators. If you already have leadership development events that attract the kind of church leader you would use as a facilitator, you can use that event and turn it into a facilitator incubator. This learning event may or may not cover the same material that you will use later on at the cluster launch conference. In our case we chose to do this in order to acquaint the facilitators with the kind of curriculum stimulus their cluster will be exposed to.

At some point during the learning event, you will want to preview the learning cluster design process. Indicate your invitation to them to serve as facilitators. Allow plenty of time for discussion and an appropriate time to respond (you might write them for a response at a later date).

The three most voiced hesitations to accepting the responsibility for becoming a facilitator need to be dealt with at this time of invitation. One, some pastors will feel inadequate to "lead" a group, especially a group of their peers. You will want to assure them that you are requesting them to serve as a group facilitator and contact person with you, not as a teacher. You also commit to them that you will coach them in the role of facilitating the group's learning processes.

The second most pressing concern expressed as a hesitation to accepting cluster leadership relates to the amount of time it will require to facilitate a group. This can present a formidable obstacle in many pastors' minds. You can best counter this objection by pointing out the benefits of group learning for the participants. Motivated learners can be led to see the shortened learning curve made possible through shared learning approaches. We have several pastors in South Carolina clusters who are pursuing Doctor of Ministry degrees (a very time-consuming project) and view the learning cluster as a chance to actually save time by creating built-in focus groups and venues for project development.

A third most frequently offered hesitation to accept responsibility as a facilitator involves the pastor's inability to think of potential participants in the cluster. This consideration, especially from church leaders who have served in their current congregation for two or more years, serves to validate the need for developing a learning cluster. Our leaders are isolated from each other! Isolated pastors and church leaders are learning handicapped. As a denominational leader you have been making notes of potential cluster participants as you have cast the vision for the process among your church leaders. Making suggestions to facilitators of potential cluster members at this point is entirely appropriate. However, do not take responsibility for recruiting the cluster away from the facilitator. The dynamic of peer mentoring begins with the recruitment process.

3. Prepare a facilitators' training event

You will want to convene your newly recruited facilitators for a half-day training event. Begin the time together by rehearsing the overview of the process. Do not underestimate the importance of this vision casting. You may have tired of hearing yourself on this subject, but the participants need to hear again the rationale of the process and the benefits they can expect to reap. These are the recruiters that will make or break the process. They need to leave fired up about the cluster learning possibilities. The documents in the appendix give you a possible agenda for this initial facilitator's meeting. When the facilitators leave this event, they should know what to do and how to do it in order to bring a learning cluster to the cluster launch conference.

4. Conduct a cluster launch conference

We like to launch the clusters at a shared learning event rather than simply encouraging the facilitators to go ahead and begin meeting when they have recruited their cluster. Consider the following benefits to a cluster launch that you conduct.

(1) The cluster launch conference allows you opportunity to cast the vision for cluster process and values. The shared experience of · the cluster participants together elevates their estimation of the importance of being a part of a new learning paradigm. The launch serves the same purpose in some regards as does the celebration event for a cell church. The participants leave the launch conference with a strong sense of being a part of something significantly larger than they are, yet something they belong to and benefit from.

(2) The shared learning of the launch conference enhances the group's learning curve at the very beginning of their experience. The learning focus goes a long way toward solidifying the cluster's agenda as a learning team rather than predominately as a support group. If the conference provides an overview of the issues the clusters will tackle, it also aids in establishing the learning agenda they will pursue. The event raises the ideas and issues for leadership development for a new apostolic era. At our conference we visit issues from each of the four areas of the balanced leadership menu identified in this book (paradigm issues, micro-skill set development, resource management, and personal life maintenance). We do this in a day and a half of conferencing. The conference can begin to prepare a new tribe of leaders within the denomination.

(3) The shared learning experience also serves as an additional way for you to touch your facilitators. No part of the denomination-ally-sponsored process is more critical than this—maintaining contact with the cluster facilitators. In our system the facilitators are invited to be a part of the whole cluster launch experience, but specifically are asked to show up for the second day of the two-day event. We conclude the formal learning sessions at noon and provide a lunch for the learning clusters to meet together to plan their initial meeting calendar and learning agenda. This captures the momentum of the two days and accelerates the cluster's develop-ment.

5. *Create learning support for lay leaders*

Creating leadership learning for key lay leaders is important for two main reasons. First, information for lay leaders about critical shifts that must occur for the church to experience renewal is in short supply. Denominational headquarters have tended to feed lay leaders mostly propaganda on denominational emphases and needs or delivered training to help them fulfill their organizational roles in the church structure. Strategic thinking and action must replace program maintenance as the chief occupation of church lay leaders. Such a shift would not eliminate church programs or denomina-tional concerns. It would introduce a level of leadership heretofore neglected in most churches and by most denominations. Only new style and new content leadership will give us different results measured in more effective church ministries.

A second reason for supplying lay leaders with learning re-sources is to support the new tribe of church leaders you are cultivating. We all know the fate of messengers, especially those who are harbingers of bad news (translated "change" in church lingo). Denominations can support church leaders by saying to their leaders what we are saying to them. Otherwise we are setting them up for certain collision with status quo forces. If denominational leaders decide to stimulate leadership development as a key plank in our strategy with lay leaders, we will forge a new coalition of leadership for a new apostolic era.

In our South Carolina system we support lay leadership learning as it relates to clusters in three ways. First, we have built the cluster constellation conference into our system. Second, we are developing a leadership tape club for key lay leaders that shares the same information we share with their pastors and staff members at our leadership conferences. This is designed as an interventionist strategy to prompt discussion and facilitate strategic reconceptualization of the church's mission at the local congregational level. Third, we produce a conference, called Kingdom Builders, for lay leaders of the congregations whose pastors or staff are members of learning clusters. This event also focuses on introducing participants to new leadership issues and approaches consonant with what we are sharing with cluster participants. This helps to seed the revolution and the rise of apostolic leadership.

6. *Some principles for any denominational system*

No matter what path you choose for developing learning communities, you will want to keep these principles in mind.

(1) Focus on leadership. Cast vision for your process, recruit facilitators, and provide these with adequate training and coaching. We are developing a more proactive strategy for contacting facilitators by newsletter, phone, and so forth as our process involves more and more clusters.

(2) Give yourself permission to start small if necessary. The process of creating learning communities is an organic one. Plant it, and give it air and vital nutrients of funding and energy. Let it grow and take shape. The idea is right. You will improve our applications for your context.

(3) Pay attention to cluster affinities in the recruiting process. More than any other single factor on the recruiting agenda this spells the recipe for disaster or celebration.

(4) Provide stimulating learning resources. This means focusing on developing up-to-date, relevant resources for leaders in the four

key issue areas we have identified. This does not mean that you must produce every single curriculum piece for clusters to use. However, you may want to provide or recommend learning resources in order to stimulate their learning. In this way you serve as a concept and resource broker for your clusters.

7. Consider other applications

The learning community process is a transferable concept that can adapt to many applications.

• Remember, you can establish learning clusters for staff positions other than that of senior pastor. These staff members would automatically be a part of the learning constellation of their pastor's learning cluster. However, church staff leaders have specialized needs of their own in the four critical issue areas common to all church leaders. They learn from colleagues who are facing similar ministry challenges and opportunities.

• Pastors of multi-staff churches can be encouraged to turn their staff into learning communities. Part of staff work would be learning and creating venues where learning debriefings can occur.

• Pastors can create learning communities of their congregational leadership core. The challenges and tasks would be to design a learning apparatus and to create venues for sharing learning insights among all leaders.

• Denominational staffs could also adopt the learning cluster model. Team members in various departments could sharpen one another's learning and debrief other staffers with their gleanings. The learning curve of the entire staff would steepen, making them a more valuable resource to each other and to the congregations in their denomination.

Once established, the learning cluster actually can serve as a delivery system for denominational leaders to supply learning resources of all kinds to the participating congregations. Ongoing research and development could be conducted among cluster churches. Denominations could introduce and even help to implement new approaches to ministry. This would position them more favorably for creating a better future for themselves and for their constituents.

11.

WHAT ABOUT SEMINARY?

Can seminaries play a role in the apostolic leadership revolution? Those entrusted with determining the future of seminary education are scrambling to script futures where seminary education remains a viable part of the credentialing process for church leaders. This search is prompted by several growing concerns and trends. More and more churches are hiring staff ministers right from the pews without any requirements for theological education. There is little wonder to this. The competencies these congregations seek are not academic. This realization has also come home to seminary graduates. Surveys show up that the overwhelming majority of them feel unprepared for the ministry challenges they face as they enter the service of churches.

Can the old academic culture be changed? Or is it better to abandon it and create a new system? Should we even expect seminaries to assume leadership development as their agenda?

One scenario calls for theological schools to attract and service a different constituency than future pastors and church workers. This trend is already well underway in many schools. A second scenario calls for twelve residential schools in the United States in 2050 serving all Protestant churches, largely through extensions or distance learning. A third calls for seminaries to specialize in training people to teach in seminaries when vacancies occur. A fourth scenario combines aspects of the previous three. A fifth scenario is to write seminaries off and create new learning communities that do not depend on people interrupting one or two careers, intentionally dislocating their families, and adopting the poverty of full-time student status in pursuit of a degree that may or may not land them a job (that will, if they get it, never allow them to economically recover from their decision to pursue a seminary education).

A sixth scenario, and the most difficult to implement, is for theological schools to become learning communities. If the learning community provides an effective process for leadership development among ministry practitioners, what about its possible role in seminary education? Can the cluster concept find a home in an academic setting? The answer: not only can this learning methodology work, it should be implemented as a better alternative than current models of seminary education.

Three Key Questions

Reengineering efforts in seminary education need to take three major paradigm shifts into account.

1. What are we about: teaching or learning?

Seminaries must shift from focusing on teaching to focusing on learning. The two pursuits can be, and often are, nonintersecting. Most current seminary schedules provide a menu of teaching times for professors to practice their lecturing. "Learning" is then measured by the students' ability to reconstruct lecture material unaided by referencing their notes (something the professor could not do when delivering the lecture). Little real correlation may exist between the classroom information exchange and genuine learning. This observation does not even take into account whether the student considered the information worth learning in the first place.

The need to reconceptualize learning is a matter that extends well beyond the concerns for theological education alone. School systems in our culture have worked from a Newtonian worldview that focuses on cause and effect, prosecuting learning by reducing subjects into parts. The belief was that if we actually understood the parts, we could understand the whole, that analysis would lead to synthesis. This has proven to be an erroneous assumption. However, it was institutionalized in the nineteenth century in a "one size fits all" educational delivery system that assumed class time and course credits as indicators of genuine understanding.

Stephanie Pace Marshall, President of the Association for Supervision and Curriculum Development, contends that a dysfunctional paradigm of learning emerged with the following set of additional, incorrect assumptions:

> Learning is passive and incremental rather than dynamic and developmental.
> Learning is acquired information, not constructed meaning. . . .
> Learning is defined by the calendar and how long one stays on the task and not by demonstration [of understanding].
> Content coverage and reproduction are more important than genuine understanding. . . .
> Content segmentation is more highly valued than concept integration.
> Reliable evaluation can only be objective and external [grades handed out by the teacher], not qualitative and self-adjusting.
> Competition is a far more powerful motivater than cooperation.[1]

All of this flies in the face of how we now know human beings learn. The competition, independence, and isolation of this current model do not stimulate the highest potential in learners. "We crave connectedness and meaning, we seek lasting and deep relationships, we grow by sharing and not by keeping secrets, and we need to trust and be trusted in order to feel safe enough to dare," Marshall asserts.[2] Both Marshall's assessment of the current educational dilemma and her plea for a corrective sound like a marketing piece for the learning cluster. "We need to create learning and teaching communities that enable learners to direct their own learning . . . to increase their intellectual, social, and emotional engagement with others; and foster collaborative and dynamic approaches to learning that enable them to develop thoughtful and integrative ways of knowing. We must create a learning culture that provides a forum for risk, novelty, experimentation . . . "[3] A new model should be

• "personalized, flexible, and coherent (learning connected to real-life issues)"

• "internally and externally networked and not bounded by physical, geographic, or temporal space"

• "accountable to the learner, adaptive to multiple learning environments"

• "interconnected and collaborative"

• "engaged in authentic dialogue with members of the internal and external community"

• "focused on inquiry, problem-solving, and problem resolution"[4]

Typical seminary education is curriculum-driven and teacher-centered. In the future professors will be held accountable for the learning of their students, not for the time they spend teaching.

2. What do we measure: course work? competence? a call to the Christian ministry? character? skills in interpersonal relationships? or Christian commitment?

Seminary degrees currently certify that a student has successfully completed a course of study that satisfies his or her degree program. In the past academic excellence in and of itself may have qualified a person to prosecute an effective ministry agenda. That this is no longer the case cannot be disputed. In that same old paradigm the student was driven by a call growing out of deep Christian commitment. Character had been tested and proved in local congregations which recommended persons to seminary for ministry preparation.

Churches would view seminary certification as more meaningful if it vouched for the graduate's having developed competencies that equip him or her to minister effectively. Seminaries will need to decide if they are willing to accept this challenge. If they are, then their graduates' capacity to demonstrate call, character, commitment, and competence will need to drive the learning efforts. The measuring standards will need to reflect these new criteria rather than counting hours spent in a seat in a classroom.

3. What are we preparing students to enter: church employment or kingdom enterprise?

In the past, students have attended seminary for credentialing to pursue a career of serving congregations in various capacities or perhaps to train for missionary or denominational service. Congregations, mission boards, and denominational agencies have largely looked to the seminary as the source of leadership training.

In the future, seminaries will continue a trend already begun at the cutting edge of theological institutions. They will train leaders for kingdom enterprise, including in their student bodies more and more learners who never intend to serve a congregation, mission board, or denominational agency in a vocational or bivocational way. These students are volunteer lay ministry leaders in congregations who want to pursue some academic study or benefit from some specialized training for their ministry leadership role. Many other future seminarians will use most of what they learn outside a local church, denominational, or institutional ministry context.

Scenarios of Cluster Implementation

Cluster learning can help seminaries explore answers to these paradigm challenges, as well as improve the learning in existing models. The following scenarios raise a few possibilities for redesigning seminaries to become learning communities for developing apostolic leaders. These scenarios do not attempt fully detailed implementation plans. They identify only the broadest contours of a new seminary training landscape that would feature cluster learning. They also assume the application of new technologies to seminary education, a process already underway in some places. Some scenarios incorporate more of the existing seminary model than do others.

Scenario 1

A student opts for residential study, arriving on seminary campus to begin a year of required interdisciplinary study. The seminary has determined that no matter what degree program students pursue, they will attend certain core competency classes. These are offered to students in classes attended by students of all schools and taught mostly by interdisciplinary faculty teams. Assignments are completed through teaching-to-learn processes supervised by the professors. This approach begins to counter the typical seminary experience that individualizes learning for people who will later serve together with other staff and lay ministry partners.

At the end of the first year, the student has discovered or chosen a small group of colleagues with whom he or she will complete seminary education. The learning cluster they become then charts a learning path that will allow them to demonstrate the competencies and mastery of information appropriate to their degree plan. The cluster designs their own schedule and determines how they will pursue their learning objectives. These may include dividing up assignments among themselves; visiting ministry venues they find intriguing; and interviewing business, community, and church leaders whose leadership skills they admire or loath. Their assignments may require the design and completion of certain ministry projects.

Curriculum for the cluster includes a variety of options. The participants may attend lectures of visiting faculty. Most prepared curriculum pieces will be obtainable through CD-ROM offerings that include lectures of professors and practitioners from all over the world, along with learning guides to help the students capture the meaning of the presentation. These can be viewed individually or corporately by cluster members. A professor is assigned to the cluster as a learning coach. He or she may meet with the group on a regular basis both to design and to monitor the learning process.

This learning cluster approach would currently be called cheating in some of its applications. However, it more closely resembles the way knowledge will be constructed in real-life ministry, done in collaboration with other staff or lay ministry colleagues. This model would also allow for the inspection and validation of a number of competencies in the learner, not just his or her academic prowess. The learning in this design is learner-driven, more fun, and more apt to deliver a graduate who is prepared to prosecute an effective ministry agenda.

Scenario 2

A student elects to take one year of the core interdisciplinary classes on seminary campus. At the end of that time she moves away from the campus, either assuming a ministry post or securing other employment. The rest of her seminary education is conducted on the field in a learning cluster. Again, she and the other cluster members can access curriculum material through CD-ROM or compressed video technology. The learning team designs their learning around ministry venues they are involved in already. Their learning is monitored by faculty or approved field coaches. When agreed upon competencies are evidenced, a certificate acknowledging completion of seminary-supervised learning is awarded.

Scenario 3

In this scenario the student never or rarely visits the campus to pursue his seminary degree. He forms a cluster with students who also are nonresident at the school campus. In some cases cluster members could be other seminarians who are geographically proximate and pursuing degrees (even from other seminaries in a seminary learning consortium). This approach could also accommodate clusters who meet on the Internet regularly and face-to-face monthly, quarterly, or infrequently if great distances separate the learners. This scenario could also allow a student to be paired not with other students but with practitioners engaged in ministry who would be willing to mentor the cluster member by participating with him in a learning community. This approach would especially be helpful for those pursuing specialized ministry or who want to combine their seminary education with other life pursuits.

Again distance learning technology combined with a CD-ROM library or Internet access could supply necessary curriculum to the clusters that become a dispersed student body. A learning coach would monitor the student's progress in ministry. Degrees would be awarded when established competencies are demonstrated. This model reinvents the seminary to become cluster-driven.

Scenario 4

In this model the learning cluster serves as a value-added dimension to more traditional seminary learning. A student could be assigned to a cluster throughout her seminary career. The level of peer mentoring may increase toward graduation, with early days involving more supervised mentoring through professors, more advanced students, or practitioners. The purpose of the cluster in this model would be more for debriefing classroom work or for spiritual formation. Learning assessments remain in typical classroom settings. Some seminaries are already applying this model in response to the cry for mentoring in spiritual formation.

Scenario 5

In this application of cluster learning only part of the seminary career includes a cluster group experience. The cluster duration could range from a semester on the front or back end to a year or more in length. The cluster function could be task-specific (preparing for comprehensive exams) or for purposes of initiation for new seminarians (with the cluster being led by a professor or more advanced classmate).

At whatever level the learning cluster model is applied to the seminary learning process, some positive benefits will emerge. The students' learning curves will go up. They will experience team-designed approaches to knowledge-building. They will be introduced to a model of learning they can then adapt or create for themselves on the field in their ministry careers. If they are fortunate enough to minister within a denomination that provides cluster learning facilitation, their early exposure to this methodology will make them more likely to engage in this form of ongoing leadership development.

The Faculty Issue

Seminaries are run, by and large, for the faculty. Anyone wanting to pursue alternative models for seminary education has to solve the faculty issue. In a learning cluster model application, what would faculty do?

• Faculty would still deliver information, even lecture, but would not deliver the same information over and over, being tied to a lectern semester after semester to give the same presentation. With current technology these presentations could be captured on video, stored on CD-ROM, and combined with interactive learning exercises that students all over the world can access.

• Faculty could spend the time spent out of the traditional classroom in other creative pursuits: research, writing new course material for elective or enrichment curriculum, travelling, teaching on distance learning networks, consulting, or being personally involved in ministry venues related to their field of interest—just to name a few possibilities.

• Faculty could assume responsibility for coaching learning clusters. This would involve helping clusters determine their learning paths and consulting them along the way on a variety of issues, including the development of appropriate projects that will result in acquired understanding. This would allow faculty to mentor, to be involved in students' lives, and to learn from their students' learnings.

• Faculty could form learning clusters with their colleagues. These clusters could be interdisciplinary, involving faculty from the same campus or from around the world. The clusters could also involve practitioners of ministry, government, education, business, or nonprofit organizations.

The Role of Administration

The seminary administration would need to make some commitments to faculty for the transition to occur to learning cluster methodology.

• Special training would need to be offered to faculty to equip them in coaching skills Most faculty have been trained to speak, to research, and to write, but not to coach. If new responsibilities revolve around coaching, they should be adequately prepared for the task.

• New reward and incentive systems would need to be devised to encourage growth in creative pursuits so that faculty would provide stimulating curriculum pieces for the learning clusters.

• Faculty would need at their disposal the necessary technology and training to make use of it. They might also need coaching for their presenting skills for video and distance learning venues.

• A transition plan would need to layer in the training and new responsibilities without creating faculty burnout.

In *Leadership and the New Science,* Margaret Wheatley contends that self-organization in natural systems will emerge from the dynamic interconnectedness of three domains: identity, information, and relationship.[5] The new work of leaders, including seminary administration, is to create the conditions whereby identity, information, and relationships are connected around the organization's larger purpose. Careful attention will need to be given to these dynamics if the learning revolution is to have a chance for success on seminary campuses.

Some would view the suggestions of this chapter as too difficult to implement. There is no question that the challenges to overhauling seminary education are formidable. The reengineering energies will have to extend beyond the usual approaches of attempting to make significant change through tinkering around with the curriculum and degree programs. More than curriculum revision is required. The delivery system must be redeveloped. The learning community approach would not only accomplish a transformation of the preparation process but would equip students for lifelong learning. It would also emphasize the priority of relationship in ministry by placing it at the heart of the learning process. A significant amount of participant self-understanding could be gained in a noncrisis setting. Faculty could find fulfillment through having time to pursue creative studies while having significant impact on students' lives, two elements presently at risk in many traditional seminary settings.

Seminaries must reinvent themselves if they intend to remain viable players in developing leaders for a new apostolic era. Those seminaries that join the leadership and learning revolution will be able to script a vibrant future for themselves.

12.

TOMORROW ARRIVED YESTERDAY

The dearth of leadership is apparent throughout society. No matter where we turn we see a severe lack of faith in the leadership of our schools, religious organizations, and governments . . . I contend that this leadership crisis is in reality a leadership development crisis. I believe that two major training and development factors have incited this crisis. First, the traditional methods used to train and educate executives have not kept pace with the monumental changes taking place in the world, and second, on-the-job experiences and development do not produce the leadership our organizations need.

—James F. Bolt[1]

These words by a prominent leadership development consultant for business confirm several central tenets of this book. First, we have a leadership crisis in our country that extends to the church. Second, we need new leadership for new challenges. We have called this apostolic leadership. Third, there is a connection between leadership development methodologies and the competence of the leadership they produce. We have contended that neither current academic nor conference learning is adequate to produce leaders for a new apostolic era. The emergence of apostolic leadership depends on a different development process than what is currently in place. The intentional creation of learning communities incorporates the dimensions of peer mentoring and knowledge-building that are essential for the development of effective apostolic leaders who can prosecute missional agendas that expand the kingdom of God.

The revolution in apostolic leadership development through learning communities is already underway. It is an idea whose time has come. When I speak on this subject, inevitably people share with me how they have implemented some aspect of this learning approach in their lives or ministries. Some are church leaders who are unable to draw on traditional sources for help in dealing with the ministry challenges they face. Others are denominational leaders who are seeking to implement some sort of clustering plan. Some of their plans are built around providing personal support for ministers while others use learning as the organizing principle for cluster development. Perhaps you yourself are already experimenting or implementing some aspect of this learning methodology. This book has been offered in hopes of speeding your journey along while enticing others to join in the adventure.

A few specific examples will serve to confirm the emergence of learning communities as a primary new vehicle for leadership development. The Lutheran Church-Missouri Synod is one of several denominational organizations seeking to implement some form of cluster development. The Developing Leaders for Ministry program (DLM) ambitiously hopes to foster learning clusters nationwide. Initially begun as a mentoring process to facilitate the emergence of metachurch congregations, the DLM project now views the learning cluster as a vehicle to facilitate peer mentoring across a wide range of leadership issues.

Other denominational efforts take on a more regional or local flavor. The West Michigan District of Wesleyan Churches has about fifty churches. A pilot project created two clusters of five churches each. They contracted with an outside consultant to provide them with guidance in such areas as the pastor's own spiritual development, cooperative intercession, spiritual disciplines for the church, lay mobilization, evangelism, and managing change. Initial success has led to plans of expanding the Congregational Clustering Program.

Seminaries are beginning to get into the act, too. The cry for mentoring has pushed seminaries all across the country to implement some form of intentional mentoring. Some link practitioners and seminarians for expanded field education. Others focus on creating campus relationships. These programs range from individual mentoring partnerships to group processing. In some schools the mentoring occurs throughout the seminarian's entire academic program. In others a student is clustered for spiritual formation, mentored initially by a more advanced student and then by a professor. As cluster learning applications grow, more and more of the educational process will take a friendlier view toward cluster methodology. The Association of Theological Schools is entertaining more creative approaches.

Denominational involvement in learning cluster development may make little difference to the highly-motivated, local church leader who is not waiting on anyone to help him or her create a learning network. However, denominational facilitation will make a great deal of difference to church leaders who do not know how to go about the process or who lack exposure to leadership resources outside their congregation or denomination. Simply by affirming the learning community concept, these denominations will raise the value of learning and empower church leaders to improve their leadership. They will sharpen the skills of their church leaders through the facilitated debriefing process that lies at the heart of the learning cluster process.

Does proof exist for making these assertions? Yes. In response to a recent questionnaire distributed to cluster participants in our South Carolina process, we received the following replies. In response to the question, "What changes have you seen in your leadership as a result of your cluster experience?" some said:

—"I am more confident."

—"I have been given permission to lead."

—"I have become more aware of the responsibility of sharing ministry responsibility with others and empowering laity to accomplish the work of ministry."

—"I have been better able to delegate."

—"I have been helped to keep a greater focus in the mission."

When asked, "What have you learned that has benefited you most personally?" we received the following replies:

—"I was going through some very serious personal problems. These men listened to me, loved and prayed for me, and carried me through a time that was ministry threatening."

—"The cluster has filled a huge void in my life—the need for deeper relationships with my peers."

—"I find security in the structure of the group and the account-ability it elicits. God is reaffirming His call on my life . . . I have (re)learned that I am not in this all alone.

—"God has used the learning cluster to lift my eyes to a wider circle of vision for the body of Christ."

—"Because we are in similar churches, I've learned from them what has worked for them and, in some cases, have been able to transfer that to my church."

These and other comments convince us that we are on to something.

Whether you are a local church pastor or staff member, a denomi-national worker, or in some other capacity of kingdom responsibil-ity, a world of improved skills and personal support awaits you in a learning community. If you are aware of cluster-type opportunities open to you, determine how to take advantage of them. If you would like to be a part of something like this, do not wait for others to develop it for you. Go for it yourself. As a prominent business philosopher says:

The world is up for re-invention in so many ways. Creativity is born in chaos. We cannot wait for great visions from great people, for they are in short supply at the end of history. It is up to us to light our own small fires in the darkness.[2]

Like first-century leaders, new apostolic leaders face a new world. The shortage of experts and an increasingly challenging ministry environment serve to place them in similar situations. Motivated by the mission, coached by the Spirit, resourced by prayer, and encouraged by each other, this new breed of church leader spells hope for the future. The path to the future will be paved by learning. The exploration of this new learning frontier for church leaders is just beginning.

Join the revolution! But first, go get three others to join you!

APPENDIX

Leadership Development Strategy
Involving Learning Clusters

Purpose: To develop a process for leadership development for pastors, staff, and key lay leaders that supplements academic and conference learning and captures experiential insights in an atmosphere of mutual encouragement.

A. Philosophical bases and core concerns

1. The need for leadership training
2. The isolation of pastors and churches
3. The debilitation of loneliness and feelings of insignificance
4. The dynamic of small group support
5. The issue of integration
6. The value of plural leadership learning
7. The vision of Empowering Kingdom Growth

B. Cluster components

1. Size: four pastors or church staff, plus their churches' leadership constellation

2. Affinities: size of church; philosophy of ministry; ministry agenda and situation; age; tenure and experience; location; and personality and temperament

3. Duration: two or three years with annual covenant renewal

4. Entry qualifications: attendance at shared learning experience; covenant commitment to accountability; confidentiality; commitment to include a plurality of church leadership in the process; willingness to produce a learning experience with others in the cluster; and covenant renewed annually

5. Cluster calendar: six to eight meetings of cluster core quartet annually and a semiannual learning event coproduced for learning constellations of the four churches

6. Cluster leadership: a facilitator (one of the quartet) selected annually by the Leadership Development Team (LDT) director; separate covenant, including expectations and benefits; and semiannual facilitator's training

7. Recruitment: combination of facilitator enlistment and volunteer interest

8. Marketing: appropriate notification in various venues; available brochure detailing process; and *Courier* article for lay information

C. Curriculum

1. Two-day entry learning event structured by LDT office

2. First year's curriculum uses parts of Joshua training; extended curriculum designed for clusters along six to eight tracs visited annually by learners

3. Curriculum pieces designed and produced by combination of South Carolina Baptist Convention staff and other resource people

D. Management

1. Facilitators coached in recruitment strategies

2. Semiannual facilitators' training provides the "pay" for assuming cluster leadership responsibilities

3. Records of cluster activity maintained in LDT office

E. Cost

1. Entry events heavily subsidized

2. Facilitators' training provided as bonus to cluster leadership

3. Curriculum production and distribution

4. Support for cluster conferences for leadership constellations

F. Distance learning possibilities

1. Satellite broadcasts for entry events delivered to learning centers (Baptist Medical Center counseling centers) with skilled facilitators on site

2. Satellite broadcasts of curriculum components delivered to learning clusters

3. Cluster constellation conferences could have video or live satellite feed as one format

4. Eventual menu of curriculum accessible by computer

G. Tracking and Measuring

1. Variables for quality growth assessed monthly
2. Expert software growth analysis available to cluster participants

H. Time line

1. Cluster process overview at Joshua Project, February
2. Facilitators' training in April
3. Formation of cluster groups by the end of June with leadership drawn from Joshua alumni
4. Cluster launch conference in August
5. Cluster celebration, the following May
6. Cluster renewal, the following summer

Learning Cluster Facilitator Covenant
Annually Renewable

As a facilitator of a learning cluster, I covenant to accept the following responsibilities:

I will recruit a learning cluster of three other pastors, bringing them to a cluster launch learning experience.

I will convene the learning cluster six to eight times annually.

I will make such reports as requested to the Leadership Development and Pastoral Ministries office.

I will plan and coordinate semiannual constellation conference events.

I will handle any group difficulties or problems in a timely and appropriate manner within the group, utilizing the Leadership Development and Pastoral Ministries Office if necessary.

Appendix

I will lead the cluster to choose a balanced plan of study, selecting at least one portion of study annually from each sector of leadership curriculum offerings.

I will commit to serving in this capacity for two years unless providentially hindered.

_____   _____

Date   Signed

Benefits of Learning Cluster Participation

1. Field-driven learning

2. Peer coaching for micro-skill development

3. Accelerated learning curve for you and your church leaders

4. Access to advanced training curriculum

5. Support group

6. Lay leaders gain access to Kingdom Builders' conferences

7. Church leaders gain exposure to ideas and concepts that put them on the same page with their pastor

Recruiting Your Learning Cluster

1. Pray about your choices.

2. The following affinity factions need to be considered in your recruitment:
   Size of congregation (worship attendance especially)
   Geography
   Church age

Length of pastor's tenure
Philosophy of ministry
Church ministry situation (mission and geography)
Personal relationship

3. Be careful to avoid recruiting VDPs (to paraphrase Gordon McDonald, Very Draining Pastors).

Build on islands of health and strength
A group *cannot* survive more than one VDP

4. Do not lower expectations in order to convince pastors to participate. Share ahead of time the expectations you have for the group.

5. Do not accept an answer immediately. Ask them to pray about their response and return a signed covenant to you.

6. Intend to enjoy this group, or you will not get together.

Cluster Enrollment Report Form

Deadline: _____

Facilitator:

Name _____

Spouse _____

    Phone   (O) _____

                (H) _____

                (FAX) _____

                Internet _____

Appendix

Participants:

1. Name_____

    Spouse_____

       Phone   (O) _____

                  (H) _____

                  (FAX) _____

                  Internet _____

2. Name _____

    Spouse _____

       Phone   (O)_____

                  (H) _____

                  (FAX) _____

                  Internet _____

3. Name_____

    Spouse_____

       Phone   (O) _____

                  (H) _____

                  (FAX) _____

                  Internet _____

CLUSTER LAUNCH SCHEDULE

Day One

8:00 - 8:30	Registration
8:30 - 10:00	Session I: Shifting Paradigms
10:00 - 10:30	Break
10:30 - Noon	Session II: Providing Leadership
Noon - 1:30	Lunch
1:30 - 3:00	Session III: Planning Kingdom Growth
3:00 - 3:30	Break
3:30 - 5:00	Session IV: Underwriting Kingdom Enterprises

Day Two

8:15 - 8:30	Devotion
8:30 - 10:00	Session V: Managing Change and Transition
10:00 - 10:30	Break
10:30 - Noon	Session VI: Keeping a Heart for Ministry
Noon - 2:00	Cluster Groups Luncheon/ Planning

Illustrated Two-Year Cluster Time Line

1999

April	Facilitator training	
June	Deadline for recruiting cluster	
August	Cluster Launch Conference	
September	Cluster meeting	Cultural trends
October	Cluster meeting	Visioning
November	Cluster meeting	Prayer
December	Facilitator training	

2000

January	Cluster meeting	Family of origin issues
February	**"CULTURAL TRENDS"**	**CONSTELLATION CONFERENCE**
March	Cluster meeting	Managing changes
April	Cluster meeting	Staff management
May	Cluster meeting	Family relationship
May 2-3	Kingdom Builders' Conference	

May	Cluster Celebration	
June-August	Couple Celebration	Couple Renewal
	Covenant Renewal	Fellowship
September	Cluster meeting	Paradigm shifts in ministry
October	**"MANAGING CHANGE"**	**CONSTELLATION CONFERENCE**
November	Cluster meeting	Money
December 4	Facilitator training	

2001

January	Cluster meeting	Personal group
February	Cluster meeting	Networking
March	**"VISIONING" CONSTELLATION CONFERENCE**	
April	Cluster meeting	Time
May	Cluster meeting	Communicating
May	Cluster Celebration	
June-August	Couple Celebration	Finishing well
	Graduation	

Illustrated Two-Year Cluster Time Line Worksheet

Topics:

1999

April	Facilitator training	
June	Deadline for recruiting cluster	
August	Cluster Launch Conference	
September	Cluster meeting	_____
October	Cluster meeting	_____
November	Cluster meeting	_____
December	Facilitator training	

2000

January	Cluster meeting	_____
February	**"CULTURAL TRENDS"**	**CONSTELLATION CONFERENCE**
March	Cluster meeting	_____
April	Cluster meeting	_____

May	Cluster meeting	_____
May 2-3	Kingdom Builders' Conference	
May	Cluster Celebration	
June-August	Couple Celebration	_____
	Covenant Renewal	_____
September	Cluster meeting	_____
October	**"MANAGING CHANGE"**	**CONSTELLATION CONFERENCE**
November	Cluster meeting	_____
December 4	Facilitator training	

2001

January	Cluster meeting	_____
February	Cluster meeting	_____
March	**"VISIONING" CONSTELLATION CONFERENCE**	
April	Cluster meeting	_____
May	Cluster meeting	_____
May	Cluster Celebration	
June-August	Couple Celebration	_____
	Graduation	

Curriculum Tracs/Menu Options
for Cluster Group Study

Paradigm Issues:
Significance of paradigms
New Testament paradigm shifts
Cultural trends forcing new paradigms
Shifts in ministry

Leadership Micro-skill Issues:
Visioning
Team building
Managing change and transition
Dealing with conflict
Mentoring and discipling
Networking
Communicating and preaching
Managing corporate cultures
Style assessment
Planning and leading worship

Resource Management Issues:
  Prayer
  Staff leadership team
  Lay ministry partners
  Money
  Time
  Facilities
  Community resources

Personal Life Issues:
  Spiritual formation
  Personal growth
  Family of origin issues
  Hidden addictions and compulsions
  Leadership dragons
  Family relationships
  Friends
  Surviving success and failure
  Finishing well
  Managing criticism

For suggested reading in each of these categories, see the bibliography at the end of this book.

SAMPLE CLUSTER MEETING

Time frame: 2-3 hours

Elements include:
  1. Fellowship
  2. Study time:
        Book reports
        Prepared papers
        Shared documents
        Case study
  3. Goal-setting and accountability
  4. Prayer time
  5. Future plans:
        Date, time, and place of next meeting
        Study assignments

CLUSTER MEETING REPORT

Facilitator: _____

Date of Report: _____

Meeting details:

Date: _____

Time: _____

Location: _____

List of attendees:

_____

_____

_____

_____

Subject for learning:

_____

Next learning topic:

_____

Comments/Requests/Challenges:

_____

_____

_____

_____

❑ Check here for Couple Celebration supplement to be sent to participants.

LEADERSHIP CONSTELLATION COMPOSITION

You may want to include the following:

- Spouses of cluster group members
- Ministry leaders
- Staff members
- Worship leaders
- Deacons
- Sunday school teachers and leaders
- Program leaders
- Mission organization leaders
- Committee leaders and members
- Informal leaders
- Emerging leaders

Cluster Constellation Conference Checklist

1. Set a date and time.
2. Determine meeting format and topic(s) for learning.
3. Divide assignments for presentations and arrangements.
4. Communicate the conference to constellation members by

   Personal letters
   Personal contacts
   Include topic of conference
   Include benefits of attending
   Include a response mechanism

5. Communicate reservations to facilitator and host church.
6. Host church makes appropriate meal or refreshment arrangements.
7. Prepare curriculum piece(s) for participants.
8. Secure audio-visual support.
9. Take reservations at conference—forward to Leadership Development Team office. (We use this as a database for invitations to Kingdom Builders' Conferences and learning events.)
10. Provide a mixer, fellowship time for the participants.
11. Arrange for some convening music.
12. Be sure that workshop activities include mixed groups from the various churches.

CONSTELLATION CONFERENCE REPORT

Facilitator: _____

Date of Report _____

Conference Details:

    Date: _____

    Time: _____

    Location: _____

    Number attending: _____

    Topic of Conference: _____

_____

_____

_____

_____

    Observations/Requests/Challenges:_____

_____

_____

_____

_____

_____

Please include a copy of:

        registrants
        curriculum
        publicity
        program (if any)

Appendix

LEARNING CLUSTER MEMBER COVENANT

I covenant to enter into a learning cluster by affirming the following intentions:

I will attend the Cluster Launch Conference.

I will participate in this learning cluster for two years unless providentially hindered.
I will involve my church leadership in this developmental process.

I will attend cluster meetings as a matter of priority, notifying my facilitator before group meeting in case attendance is not possible.

I will complete group study assignments.

I will commit to confidentiality of group discussions.

I will participate and lead my church leaders to participate in semiannual multi-congregational conference learning events.

I will fulfill my responsibilities/assignments related to constellation conferences.
I will pray for the other members of my group on a regular basis.

_____ Signed

_____ Signed

_____ Signed

Date _____   _____Signed

NOTES

Introduction

1. Warren Bennis, "The Leader as Storyteller," *The Harvard Business Review,* January-February 1996, p. 154.
2. George Barna, *Today's Pastor* (Ventura, Calif.: Regal Books, 1993), pp. 122-24.
3. Bill Hybels, "Up to the Challenge," *Leadership,* Fall 1996, p. 56.
4. Peter Drucker, *Leader of the Future: New Essays by World-Class Leaders and Thinkers,* ed. Frances Hesselbein et al. (San Francisco: Jossey-Bass, 1996), p. xi.

1. Apostolic Leadership

1. Rodney Stark, *The Rise of Christianity* (Princeton, N.J.: Princeton University Press), p. 7.
2. George G. Hunter III, "Church for the Unchurched," *Next,* August 1996, pp. 1-3. For Hunter's full treatment of the apostolic congregation, see his *How to Reach Secular People* (Nashville: Abingdon Press, 1992) and *Church for the Unchurched* (Nashville: Abingdon Press, 1996).

3. The Case for the Learning Community

1. Based on Peter Senge, *The Fifth Discipline* (New York: Doubleday, 1990). In this volume the author identifies the essential components of a learning organization. This definition builds on this concept by highlighting some distinct ingredients that would characterize a learning community.

6. Paradigm Issues

1. Carol Childress, "Key Paradigm Questions for Churches," *Netfax* 11 (23 January 1995): 1.

7. Leadership Micro-skills

1. James M. Kouzes and Barry Z. Posner, *The Leadership Challenge* (San Francisco: Jossey-Bass, 1995), p. 199.
2. George Barna, *The Power of Vision* (Ventura, Calif.: Regal Books, 1992).
3. Burt Nanus, *Visionary Leadership* (San Francisco: Jossey-Bass, 1992).
4. Bob Wall, Robert Solum, and Mark Sobol, *The Visionary Leader* (Rocklin, Calif.: Prima Publishing, 1992).

8. Resource Management

1. Kennon Callahan, *Effective Church Finances* (San Francisco: HarperCollins, 1992), p. 31.
2. See Lyle Schaller, *44 Ways to Expand the Financial Base of Your Local Congregation* (Nashville: Abingdon Press, 1989).

9. The Leader as a Person

1. See Roy Oswald, *Clergy Self-Care: Finding a Balance for Effective Ministry* (Bethesda, Md.: Alban Institute, 1991).
2. See Daryl E. Quick, *The Healing Journey for Adult Children of Alcoholism* (Downers Grove, Ill.: InterVarsity Press, 1990), for an excellent treatment of this subject. See also Charles L. Whitfield, *Healing the Child Within* (Deerfield Beach, Fla.: Health Communications, 1987).

11. What About Seminary?

1. Stephanie Pace Marshall, "Creating Sustainable Learning Communities for the Twenty-First Century," in *The Organization of the Future,* ed. Frances Hesselbein, Marshall Goldsmith, and Richard Beckhard (San Francisco: Jossey-Bass, 1996), p. 180.
2. Ibid., p. 180-81.
3. Ibid., p. 183.
4. Margaret J. Wheatley, *Leadership and the New Science* (San Francisco: Berrett-Koehler, 1994), pp. 139-147.

12. Tomorrow Arrived Yesterday

1. James F. Bolt, "Developing Three-Dimensional Leaders," *Leader of the Future: New Essays by World-Class Leaders and Thinkers,* ed. Frances Hesselbein et al. (San Francisco: Jossey-Bass, 1996), p. 163.
2. Charles Handy, *The Age of Paradox* (Boston: Harvard Business School Press, 1994), p. 286.

BIBLIOGRAPHY

Paradigm Issues

Anderson, Leith. *Dying for Change*. Minneapolis: Bethany House, 1992.
Barker, Joel. *Future Edge: Discovering the New Paradigms of Success*. New York: William Morrow, 1992.
Callahan, Kennon L. *Effective Church Leadership*. San Francisco: Harper San Francisco, 1990.
Carter, Stephen L. *The Culture of Disbelief: How American Law and Politics Trivialize Religious Devotion*. New York: Anchor Books, 1994.
Davis, Stanley M. *Future Perfect*. Reading, Mass.: Addison-Wesley, 1989.
Hamel, Gary, and C. K. Prahaled. *Competing for the Future*. Boston: Harvard Business School Press, 1996.
Handy, Charles. *The Age of Paradox*. New York: McGraw, 1995.
Hauerwas, Stanley and William H. Willimon. *Resident Aliens*. Nashville: Abingdon Press, 1989.
Mead, Loren B. *The Once and Future Church*. Bethesda, Md.: The Alban Institute, 1991.
Morganthaler, Sally. *Worship Evangelism*. Grand Rapids: Zondervan, 1996.
Schaller, Lyle. *The New Reformation: Tomorrow Arrived Yesterday*. Nashville: Abingdon Press, 1996.

Schultz, Thom, and Joani Schultz. *Why Nobody Learns Much of Anything at Church: And How to Fix It.* Loveland, Colo.: Group, 1993.

Snyder, Howard A. *Liberating the Church.* Downers Grove, Ill.: InterVarsity, 1983.

Tucker, Robert B. *Managing the Future.* New York: Berkley Trade, 1991.

Waitley, Denis. *Empires of the Mind: Lessons to Lead and Succeed in a Knowledge-Based World.* New York: William Morrow, 1996.

Leadership Micro-skills

Barna, George. *The Power of Vision: How You Can Capture and Apply God's Vision for Your Ministry.* Ventura, Calif.: Regal Books, 1992.

Bennis, Warren, and Bert Nanus. *Leaders: The Strategies for Taking Charge.* New York: HarperCollins, 1986.

——— *Learning to Lead: A Workbook On Becoming A Leader.* Reading, Mass.: Addison-Wesley, 1994.

——— *On Becoming a Leader.* Reading, Mass.: Addison-Wesley, 1990.

——— *Why Leaders Can't Lead: The Unconscious Conspiracy Continues.* San Francisco: Jossey-Bass, 1990.

Block, Peter *Stewardship: Choosing Service over Self-Interest.* San Francisco: Berrett-Koehler, 1996.

Drucker Foundation. *The Organization of the Future.* San Francisco: Jossey-Bass, 1996.

Drucker, Peter F. *Managing the Non-Profit Organization: Principles and Practices.* New York: Harper Business, 1992.

DuPree, Max. *Leadership Jazz: The Art of Conducting Business Through Leadership, Followership, Teamwork Voice, Touch.* New York: Dell, 1993.

Finzel, Hans. *The Top Ten Mistakes Leaders Make.* Wheaton, Ill.: Victor Books, 1994.

Ford, Leighton. *Transforming Leadership: Jesus' Way of Creating Vision, Shaping Values and Empowering Change.* Downers Grove, Ill.: InterVarsity, 1993.

Gardner, John W. *On Leadership.* New York: The Free Press, 1993.

Hesselbein, Frances, et al., eds. *The Leader of the Future: New Essays by World-Class Leaders and Thinkers.* San Francisco: Jossey-Bass, 1996.

Katzenbach, Jon R., and Douglas K Smith. *The Wisdom of Teams.* Boston: Harvard Business School Press, 1993.

Kouzes, James and Barry Posner. *Credibility: How Leaders Gain and Lose It, Why People Demand It.* San Francisco: Jossey-Bass Publishers, 1993.

Nanus, Burt. *Visionary Leadership: Creating a Compelling Sense of Direction for Your Organization.* San Francisco: Jossey-Bass Publishers, 1992.

Oakley, Ed, and Doug Krug. *Enlightened Leadership.* New York: Simon & Schuster, 1994.

Peters, Tom. *The Pursuit of Wow! Every Person's Guide to Topsy-Turvy Times.* New York: Vintage, 1995.

Wall, Bob, Robert Solum, and Mark Sobol. *The Visionary Leader: From Mission Statement to a Thriving Organization, Here's Your Blueprint.* Rocklin, Calif.: Prima Publishing, 1994.

Change and Conflict

Albrecht, Karl. *The Northbound Train: Finding the Purpose, Setting the Direction, Shaping the Destiny of Your Organization.* New York: American Management Association, 1994.

Bridges, William. *Managing Transitions: Making the Most of Change.* Reading, Mass.: Addison-Wesley, 1991.

Callahan, Kenneth L. *Twelve Keys to an Effective Church.* San Francisco: HarperSan Francisco, 1983.

Clifton, Donald, and Paula Nelson. *Soar With Your Strengths.* New York: Dell, 1996.

Dobson, Edward G., Speed B. Leas, and Marshall Shelly. *Mastering Conflict and Controversy.* Sisters, Ore.: Multnomah, 1992.

George, Carl F. and Robert E. Logan. *Leading and Managing Your Church.* Ada, Mich: Fleming Revell, 1988.

Mead, Loren B. *More Than Numbers: The Ways Churches Grow.* Bethesda, Md.: The Alban Institute, 1993.

Murphy, Emmett. *The Genius of Sitting Bull: 13 Heroic Strategies for Today's Business Leaders.* Englewood Cliffs, N.J.: Prentice Hall, 1995.

O'Toole, James. *Leading Change: Overcoming the Ideology of Comfort and the Tyranny of Custom.* San Francisco: Jossey-Bass, 1996.

Robert, Michel. *Strategy Pure and Simple: How Winning CEOs Outthink Their Competition.* New York: McGraw-Hill, 1993.

Schaller, Lyle E. *44 Steps Up Off the Plateau.* Nashville: Abingdon Press, 1993.

———— *Strategies for Change.* Nashville: Abingdon Press, 1993.

Scott, Cynthia D., and Dennis T. Jaffe. *Managing Organizational Change* Menlo Park: Crisp Publications, 1989.

————, and Dennis T. Jaffe. *Managing Personal Change.* Menlo Park: Crisp Publications, 1989.

Resource Management Issues

Asimakoupoulou, Greg, Steve McKinley, and John Maxwell. *The Time Crunch: What To Do When You Can't Do It All.* Sisters, Ore.: Multnomah Press, 1993.

Barna, George. *Evangelism That Works: How to Reach Changing Generations with the Unchanging Gospel.* Ventura, Calif.: Regal Books, 1995.

Bugbee, Bruce L., et al. *The Network: Vision and Consultant.* Grand Rapids: Zondervan Publishing House, 1994.

Callahan, Kennon. *Effective Church Finances: Fund Raising and Budgeting for Church Leaders.* San Francisco: HarperSan Francisco, 1993.

——— *Giving and Stewardship In An Effective Church.* Harper San Francisco, 1992.

Jacobs, Cindy. *Possessing the Gates of the Enemy: A Training Manual for Militant Intercession.* 2nd edition. Ada, Mich.: Choosen Books, 1994.

Mackenzie, Alec. *The Time Trap.* New York: American Management Association, 1991.

Schaller, Lyle E. *44 Ways to Increase Church Attendance.* Nashville: Abingdon Press, 1987.

——— *44 Ways to Expand the Financial Base of Your Congregation.* Nashville: Abingdon Press, 1989.

Stevens, R. Paul. *The Equipper's Guide to Every-Member Ministry.* Downers Grove, Ill.: InterVarsity Press, 1992.

——— *Liberating the Laity: Equipping All the Saints for the Ministry.* Downers Grove, Ill.: InterVarsity Press, 1985.

Personal Life Issues

Barna, George. *Today's Pastors: A Revealing Look at What Pastors Are Saying About Themselves, Their Peers, and the Pressures They Face.* Ventura, Calif.: Regal Books, 1993.

Briscoe, Stuart, Knute Larson, and Larry Osborne. *Measuring Up: The Need to Succeed and the Fear of Failure.* Sisters, Ore.: Multnomah Press, 1993.

Clinton, Robert J. *The Making of A Leader: Recognizing the Stages of Leadership Development.* Colorado Springs, Colo.: NavPress, 1988.

Cloud, Henry, and John Townsend. *Boundaries.* Grand Rapids: Zondervan, 1995.

Covey, Stephen R., A. Roger Merrill, and Rebecca R. Merrill. *First Things First.* New York: Simon and Schuster, 1996.

Covey, Stephen R. *The Seven Habits of Highly Effective People.* New York: Simon and Schuster, 1989.

Dobson, Ed, Wayne Gordon, and Louis McBurney. *Standing Fast: Ministry in an Unfriendly World* Sisters, Ore.: Multnomah Books, 1994.

Dunnam, Maxie, Gordon MacDonald, and Donald McCullough. *Mastering Personal Growth.* Sisters, Ore.: Multnomah Press, 1992.

Harley, Willard F. *His Needs . . . Her Needs.* Ada, Mich.: Fleming Revell, 1986.

Hart, Archibald. *Adrenalin and Stress. Revised edition. Dallas: Word, 1995.*

——— *Healing Life's Hidden Addictions.* Ann Arbor, Mich.: Servant Publications, 1990.

London, H. B., Jr., and Neil B. Wiseman. *The Heart of A Great Pastor: How to Grow Strong and Thrive Wherever God Has Planted You.* Ventura, Calif.: Regal Books, 1994.

——— and Neil B. Wiseman. *Pastors at Risk.* Wheaton, Ill.: Victor Books, 1993.

MacDonald, Gordon. *Ordering Your Private World.* Nashville: Nelson, 1985.

——— *When Men Think Private Thoughts.* Nashville: Nelson, 1996.

Minirth, Frank and Meier, Paul. *How to Beat Burnout: Help for Men and Women.* Chicago: Moody, 1986.

Shula, Don, and Ken Blanchard. *Everyone's a Coach.* Grand Rapids: Zondervan, 1995.

Smalley, Gary, and John Trent. *The Blessing.* New York: Pocket Books, 1990.

Stanley, Paul D., and J. Robert Clinton. *Connecting: The Mentoring Relationships You Need to Succeed in Life.* Colorado Springs, Colo.: NavPress, 1992.

Swenson, Richard A. *Margins: How To Create the Emotional, Physical, Financial, and Time Reserves You Need.* Colorado Springs, Colo.: NavPress, 1995.